SADOMANIA

Glitter books

SADOMANIA

ISBN 978-1-902588-20-9
Published 2012 by Glitter Books
Edited and compiled by Jack Hunter

CULT MOVIE FILES

Introduction

ALL THE SINS OF SODOM

Biographical Note

The Marquis de Sade (1740–1814) is perhaps the most extreme example – even more so than others like Edgar Allan Poe or Oscar Wilde – of a writer whose actual life history has been inextricably confused with the events and characters depicted in his fiction, resulting in the popular perception of de Sade as some mythic personification of sexual depravity, cruelty and evil[1]. **Sadomania** investigates the zone where de Sade's life, literature and legend most closely collide with cinema.

A full account of de Sade's life, times, works and pathology can be found in Dr. Iwan Bloch's comprehensive study *De Sade: Life And Works*, but the salient points are as follows.

The Marquis de Sade was only ever convicted of two, relatively minor offences, yet due to political power-plays by his enemies, spent over 27 years of his life in prison and died in an insane asylum.

In 1768, de Sade procured a young Swiss girl, Rosa Keller, and locked her up in his *petit maison*[2]. His first action was to make her strip naked, after which he whipped her and then put a healing balm on the welts. The next day he inflicted several superficial knife-wounds on her body. She later escaped. For this admittedly unpleasant but, for the times, not entirely unusual conduct he was fined and imprisoned for 6 weeks in Saumur castle.

Far more serious consequences resulted from the second scandal of de Sade's career, the "spanish fly" affair, in 1772. The Marquis threw a ball in Marseilles, and fed his guests a chocolate dessert heavily laced with cantharide, a potent aphrodisiac. A sexual revelry – the extent of which remains unclear – ensued. Again, this event was reported with hyperbolic bias. Most reports depicted a mass orgy of Bacchanalian proportion, others adding that several guests went mad and leapt to their death from high windows. As a result, de Sade was charged with poisoning – compounded by a further charge of sodomy – and sentenced to death. The death sentence was eventually overturned, but not before de Sade had fled France. From then on, he led the life of a fugitive and was lengthily imprisoned on several separate occasions, notably at Vincennes, the Bastille, and finally at Charenton. It was in prison that de Sade wrote the pornographic epics for which he is notorious.

Time and the constant re-telling have turned both these incidents into myth. Even contemporaries of de Sade's, such as Restif de la Bretonne[3], exaggerated their journalistic reports. In Restif's version of the Keller affair, the girl found herself tied up in a dissecting theatre ready to be flayed alive, and saw the corpses of two previous victims already hanging there. Another report suggested that de Sade, rather than administering ointment to Keller's injuries, poured boiling wax into them. And so on. Thence springs the legend of de Sade the whip-wielding psychopath, forever flagellating or cutting up naked girls in some gloomy dungeon.

The primary, and permanent result of these legends was the coining, in the 19th century, of the term "sadism" to describe a psycho-sexual disorder whereby sexual arousal or gratification is obtained only by inflicting pain on others. Krafft-Ebing, in his

Psychopathia Sexualis of 1898, described many such case histories, while Iwan Bloch a year later was the first to publish a complete psychopathology of the complex as it related directly to its progenitor, the Marquis[4].

"Sadism" As Crowd-Puller

Just as the term "surreal" has been totally devalued and is now used in common parlance to describe any slightly unusual event or circumstance, so the term "sadistic" has also passed from psychological to everyday usage, and is used to describe pretty much any form of violence or cruelty, regardless of whether sexual gratification is involved. In the cinema of the 1950s and 60s, B-movie directors were quick to incorporate "sadism" into their titles, often purely for the lurid shock value and prurient interest the term could generate. For example: *The Sadist* (1963). Directed by James Landis, this is actually the tale of a pair of murdering teenagers, and is based on the true story of 50s teen spree killer Charles Starkweather; while Al Adamson's *Satan's Sadists* (1969) is no more than a violent biker movie. Greg Coranto's *Wanda The Sadistic Hypnotist* (1969) is an LSD movie with a few bondage scenes thrown in. The publicity blurb for the tame mondo film *Sadismo* (1967) declared: "Actually filmed in the dark corners of this sick world! An authentic catalog of cruelty! See The Rack/Thumb Screw/Iron Maiden/Torture Drugs That Make Men Slaves/Bizarre Human Sacrifices...Today!"; and Harald Reinl's horror *Die Schlangengrübe Und Das Pendel* (1967, aka *Castle Of The Walking Dead* aka *The Blood Demon*) was speculatively re-named *The Torture Chamber Of Dr. Sadism* for US TV. More accurately titled was George Gunter's *The Sadistic Lover* (1966), in which a peeping tom confesses to violent acts of murder and rape.

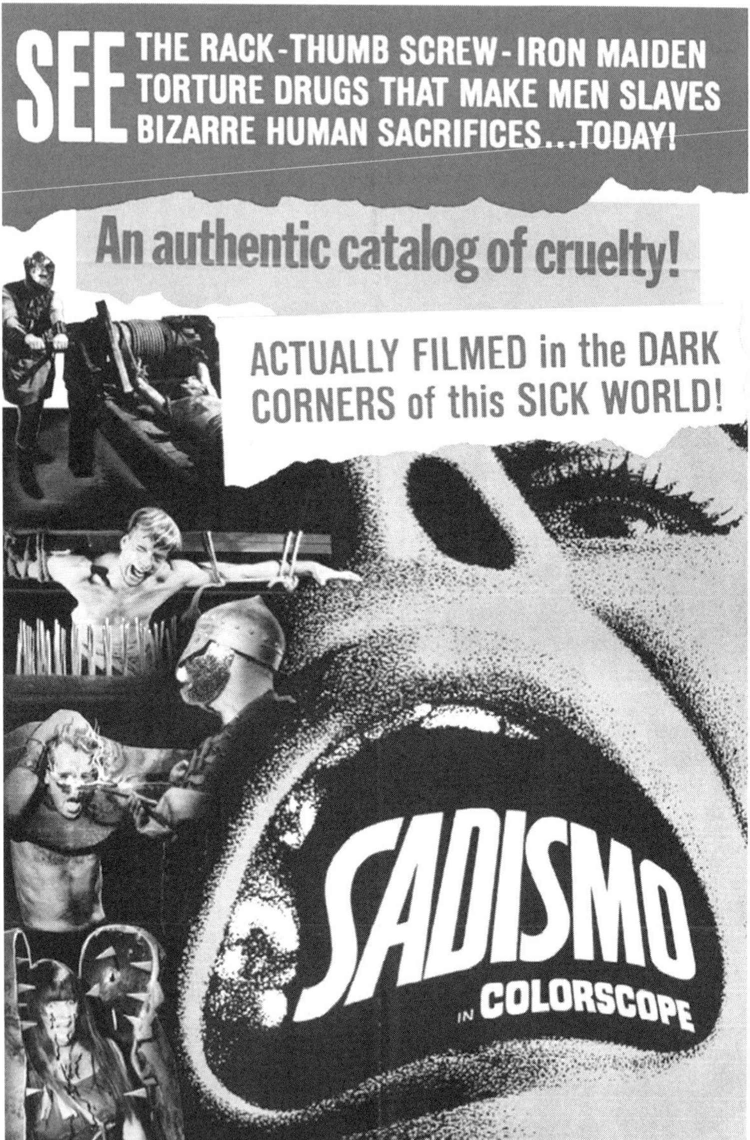
SEE
THE RACK-THUMB SCREW-IRON MAIDEN
TORTURE DRUGS THAT MAKE MEN SLAVES
BIZARRE HUMAN SACRIFICES...TODAY!
An authentic catalog of cruelty!
ACTUALLY FILMED in the DARK
CORNERS of this SICK WORLD!
SADISMO
IN COLORSCOPE

Horror

Two horror films more directly concerned with de Sade are *The Skull* (Freddie Francis, 1965) and *Night Terrors* (Tobe Hooper, 1995)[5]. *The Skull*, an Amicus production based on the Robert Bloch short story "The Skull Of The Marquis de Sade", was directed by Freddie Francis and stars Peter Cushing as Maitland, a collector of outré arcana who acquires the ultimate artefact – the skull of the Marquis de Sade. Christopher Lee plays the friend who possesses the skull of the Marquis, which Maitland greatly covets. Lee, however, warns his friend about it, claiming that it has a certain malign power and that de Sade was a Satanist who "practiced sorcery, making sacrifices of blood to his master the Devil". At this point the skull is stolen by a crooked dealer, who lives in a dismal flat and sells artefacts such as a book bound in human skin. He sells Maitland the stolen skull. With the skull in his possession, Maitland starts to behave oddly, and breaks into Lee's house in search of some recently acquired gargoyles. In a struggle, Lee is killed, and the dealer attempts to blackmail the hapless and possessed Maitland. This proves fatal, as he soon dies spectacularly, plunging through a patterned stained glass skylight in his lodgings. Suddenly, a slightly sinister film takes a dive into the unknown, as Maitland is grabbed from his house by a pair of policemen and deposited at a judge's house, where he encounters a number of strange and surreal trials, including rooms filled with gas and psychedelic lights. This bizarre section was evidently added by the producers when they realised that the story would not last feature length. Teased into the narrative with pieces of other footage, it turns a routine chiller towards surrealistic nightmare, so much so that the film's ending – where Maitland is killed, throat torn out by the spirit of the animated skull before the police can catch up with him – comes almost as an anti-climax.

Night Terrors stars Robert "Freddie Kreuger" Englund in a dual role as both the Marquis de Sade and his descendent Paul Chevalier, the master of a sinister sadean cult in present-day Egypt. Parallel narratives depict de Sade locked away in the Bastille, where he is portrayed as some kind of 18th century Hannibal Lecter, and Chevalier's somewhat tame cult orgies. Chevalier, with the help of his perverted consort Sabine, is bent on depraving an archaeologist's daughter (named Genie in a nod to Eugenie in de Sade's *Philosophy In The Boudoir*). Genie is also a dead ringer for de Sade's wife. The film weaves fantasy and reality, past and present, culminating in two climactic scenes: on the point of blinding Genie, whom he has in chains, Chevalier is stabbed by Sabine, who frees Genie before being stabbed by Chevalier in turn. And back in the Bastille, the dying de Sade's last act is to spit blood in the face of a priest (the scenes with the Marquis are far more entertaining, though fewer in number).

Little-known in Hooper's filmography (he was actually second-choice director after Gerry O'Hara), *Night Terrors* is something of a an anomaly, an uneven fusion of horror (nightmares, blindings, decapitations) and druggy softcore sleaze, Englund playing both his roles with Krueger-like relish.

Hardcore

Just as B-movie directors in the '60s used the name of de Sade to drum up sales, so the makers of hardcore porn from the '70s onwards have used the same trick of sleaze by association[6]. Following on from short stag-type films such as *Les Filles de Sade* (France, 1969) and the gay porno *Frankenstein de Sade* (USA, 1969), the Mitchell brothers (directors of the classic *Behind The Green Door*) were probably the first to produce a feature with *Beyond de Sade* (USA, 1973), which starred their protegée

Marilyn Chambers. Porno legend Alex de Renzy soon followed with *Femmes de Sade* (USA, 1977). Although this is one of de Renzy's most interesting films, filled with bizarre hardcore action (including self-fellatio), there is no real reference to the Divine Marquis. Rocky de Sade, a newly released convict, goes on a spree of misogynistic violence before getting his come-uppance at a psychedelic fancy-dress orgy, where he is chained up while his victims piss and shit on him.

Two movies from the "golden age" of porn to exploit the de Sade brand more specifically were Joe Davian's *House Of De Sade*, USA, 1977) and Phil Prince's *Kneel Before Me* (USA, 1983), both depicting sadistic extremes within a hardcore framework with specific reference to the Marquis himself. Both films are productions by Avon, the New York company which from 1975 specialised in sado-masochistic 60-minute "roughies" such as *Daughters Of Discipline* (1976), *Pornocopia Sexualis* (1977), *Revenge And Punishment* (1977), *Painmania* (1981), and *Savage Sadists* (1981), many of them directed by Joe Davian[7]. Davian was part of a cadre of Israeli pornographers, and sported a tattoo from Dachau death camp. His trademark line of films were sleazy snapshots from New York's underbelly marked by SM scenes often shot in intense gynecological detail.

House Of De Sade's vestigial plot involves a group of swingers who convene in a haunted house where they hold a naked seance to invoke the spirit of the Marquis de Sade. The leader of the group is possessed by de Sade – signified by his donning a leather mask – and proceeds to "torture" Vanessa del Rio with flagellation and nipple-clamping, aided by the drooling imbecile "butler", while the rest of the group indulge in an orgy. "You really *are* the master!" gushes Vanessa as this glorified stag movie spasms to a close.

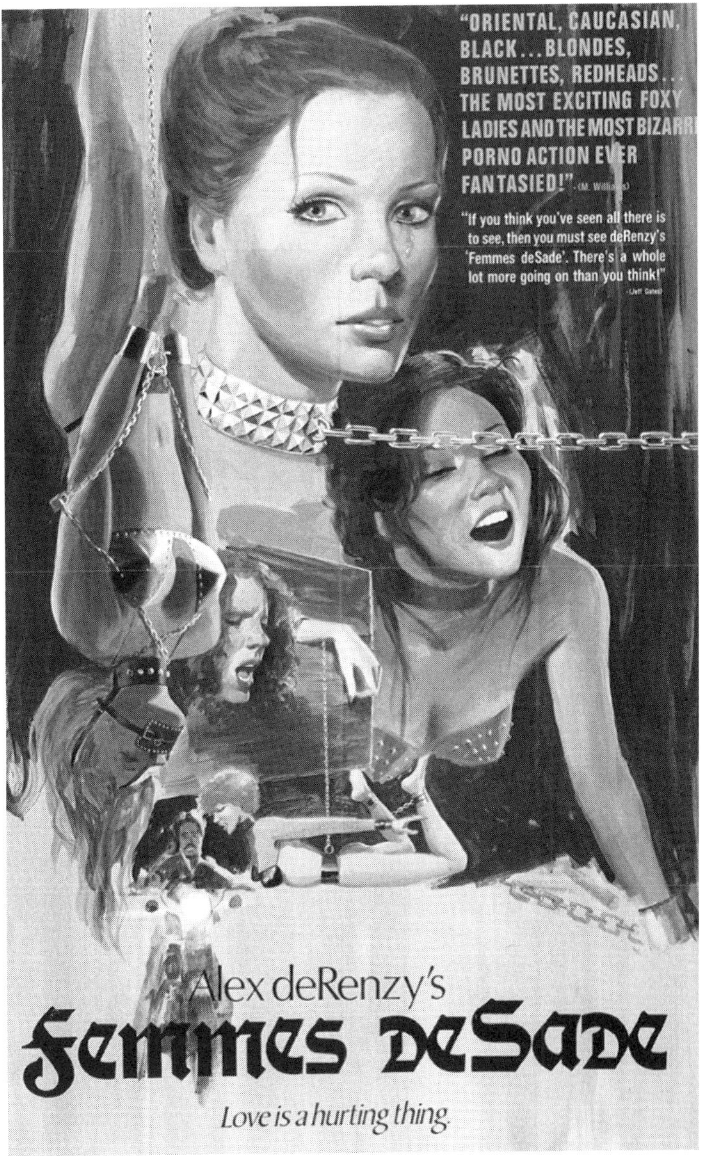
"ORIENTAL, CAUCASIAN, BLACK...BLONDES, BRUNETTES, REDHEADS... THE MOST EXCITING FOXY LADIES AND THE MOST BIZARR PORNO ACTION EVER FANTASIED!"
"If you think you've seen all there is to see, then you must see deRenzy's 'Femmes deSade'. There's a whole lot more going on than you think!"
Alex deRenzy's
Femmes deSade
Love is a hurting thing.

Phil Prince (aka Prinz), director of *Kneel Before Me*, was even more notorious than Davian, both for his films and private life (he was prime suspect in his wife's murder and later jailed for armed robbery)[8]. *Kneel Before Me*, featuring regulars Annie Sprinkle(s) and George Payne and with a supporting cast which includes Niko and Ron Jeremy, is typical of Prince's work. Again, the "plot" is negligible, though *Kneel Before Me* is more of a film than *House Of De Sad*e. A newly-wed man is plagued by vivid dreams in which he and his wife are involved in scenes of bondage, torture, orgiastic sex and murder; in the dreams he calls her "Justine", while she addresses him as "Marquis de Sade". As before, he wears a leather hood in these sequences, which comprise most of the movie and are weirdly soundtracked by slaughterhouse noises, amplified heartbeats, chanting and samples from such movies as *Halloween*. The man goes to his (female) psychiatrist who regresses him under hypnosis, revealing that he is in fact a descendent of the Marquis. Finally we also learn that the shrink is a descendent of one of de Sade's victims, seeking revenge after "three generations". On his next visit she chloroforms him; he wakes up in the dream-dungeon, tied to one of the crosses previously used to torture his victims. After jointly fellating him, the psychiatrist and the man's wife either kill or castrate him – which, is unclear. The credits roll as the bloody knife rises and falls...

Other name-dropping hardcore films and videos include: *Monsieur de Sade* (France, 1976); *China de Sade* (Charles de Santos, USA, 1977); *Mod de Sade* (USA,, 1978); *Madame de Sade's Castle Of Pleasures* (France, 1984); *Comte de Sade* (Germany, 1985); *De Sade* (Buck Adams, USA, 1987); *Villa de Sade* (USA, 1990); *Power Of de Sade* (USA, 1991); *Ménage de Sade* (USA, 1992); *Exzesse de Sade* (Germany, 1992); *Dungeon de Sade*

(USA, 1993); *Maximum de Sade* (Rick Masters, USA, 1994); *The Contessa de Sade* (Harold Lime, USA, 1996); *Madame de Sade's Dungeon* (USA, 1997); and *"M" de Sade* (Germany, 2000). Few of these films have anything to do with de Sade beyond the use of his name – Frank Zee's *The Divine Marquis* (1995), for example, offers nothing more than an old man torturing four bondage models – although the "plot" of *Maximum de Sade* does at least have the Marquis magically reincarnated in modern times. *Club Sadismo* (USA, 1992) and *Sperma-Sadismus!* (Germany, 2001) are equally irrelevant. Final mention here goes to *Forbidden Fantasies* (1992), in which Kym Wilde fantasises about the Marquis's whip.[9]

It remains a pity that no serious, authentic hardcore film version has yet been made of any of de Sade's books; for hardcore is the only genre which could truly replicate the relentless repetition of explicit sexual acts and atrocities – leavened by philosophical tracts – which make up the fabric of the texts. This section ends with a mention of one film which does, at least, boast the same combination of hardcore sex and bloody mutilation/murder as the final parts of de Sade's most extreme work, *120 Days Of Sodom*. The film is Michael Hugo's *Hardgore* (aka *Sado-Asylum*, 1973). This bizarre film is set in a remote sanatorium, where a young girl has come to be cured of "nymphomania with masochistic tendencies". The action is described as follows: "Young Maria is sent to Fox Hollows Sanitarium for treatment. During the day, sexy nurses pamper her with dildo therapy. At night Maria unwillingly participates in sex and death rituals practiced by resident cultists. A nurse has her throat slit while Maria attends a castration gang-bang. The 'ultimate orgasm' is achieved by combining sex and death! An executioner fucks a hot nurse from behind, her body locked tight in a pillory. At the moment of orgasm, cum slathers her ass and the guillotine blade severs her head. Maria is taken to 'the room', a blood drenched cadavery where skulls bleed and hot red dildos spurt thick strands of semen.... a place of meathooks, blood stains and necrophilia". Which about sums it up; *Hardgore* could be viewed as *Philosophy in The Boudoir* re-staged in a hospital, and minus the philosophy, but its technical shortcomings ultimately relegate it to the second tier of sadean cinema.

"Sadean" Cinema

Ado Kyrou, in his study *Amour-Erotisme Et Cinéma* (1957), hinted at a body of film where sadism in its truer meaning could be found – not just films of cruelty, but films where cruelty specifically leads to sexual arousal; such films are now commonly known as "sadean". Georges de Coulteray elaborated on this in his subsequent book *Sadism In The Cinema*, which was banned when first published in the US in 1964. Some primary examples of this sadean cinema include: *The Most Dangerous Game* (1932); *Peeping Tom* (1960); and Mario Bava's *The Whip And The Body* (1964).

The Most Dangerous Game is a horror film of considerable cruelty both physical and philosophical, in which Count Zaroff (played by Leslie Banks) hunts human prey on a deserted island and mounts their severed heads in his trophy room; but the sadean crux of the film comes in a declaration from Zaroff which makes it explicit that he can only achieve sexual arousal through murder: "First pursue your enemy, then pursue woman. Only after the kill, can man know the true ecstasies of love". This most classic of storylines has been reprised many times over, in such subsequent films as *A Game Of Death* (1945), *Run For The Sun* (1956), *Bloodlust!* (1961), Jesus Franco's *The*

Perverted Countess (1973), and *Seven Women For A Sadist* (1976).

Peeping Tom was directed by distinguished British director Michael Powell, and its controversial nature virtually ruined his thereto glittering career. A lurid commingling of striptease, sadism and snuff, *Peeping Tom* tells of a young photographer who uses a spiked camera tripod to murder his female victims as he films them, recording their death throes on camera. It is clear here that sexual arousal brings on the desire to kill, and that killing leads to climax. The film also works as a telling comment on voyeurism, with the viewer being implicated as much as the murderer himself.

The Whip And The Body belongs to that lurid corpus of early 60s Italian horror cinema in which sado-masochistic (not to mention necrophiliac) elements run riot, reaching a climax of sorts

in Massimo Pupillo's *Il Boia Scarlatto* (1965, aka *The Bloody Pit Of Horror*), which opens with the following "quote" in bloody lettering: *"My vengeance needs blood! –The Marquis de Sade"*.

In *The Whip And The Body*, a more subtly engaging film, Christopher Lee plays a revenant who savagely whips his lover (Dahlia Lavi) on a nightly basis, and whose penchant for sadistic sex previously led to the death of a servant girl. Bava's phantasmal colour schemata enhance the oneiric sex-violence to the point of delirium.

This Italian vogue for "sadistic" violence by men against women continued into the *giallo* genre of the latter 60s and 70s, of which the more extreme examples include *Gore In Venice* (Mario Landi, 1979), Ruggero Deodato's *House On The Edge Of The Park* (1980), and *The New York Ripper* (Lucio Fulci, 1982).

In cinema, as in history, examples of the female sadist are far less common. *Ilsa, She-Wolf Of The SS* (1974) seems to be one woman who, aided and abetted by her topless female adjutants, derives sexual gratification from inflicting humiliation, torture and even mutilation (castration); another is Madame Olga – who "possessed a mind so warped she made sadism a full-time business!" – as featured in *White Slaves of Chinatown* (1964) and its various sequels[10]. They should not be confused with the female protagonists of revenge flicks like *I Spit On Your Grave* or *Death Weekend*, who are motivated to maim purely by the desire for retribution, or those of *Repulsion* or *Possession*, who are just plain crazy.

All of the above examples, of course, come only from the world of "legitimate" (or semi-legitimate) cinema. Ever since the dawn of the stag movie, and in every country, pornographic films have been produced where naked girls are tortured for the sexual gratification of men. To list the thousands (millions?) of bondage, torture, rape or snuff films that have been produced would be both pointless and impossible; the main scope of **Sadomania**, therefore, has necessarily been narrowed to films that are partially or entirely based either on the writings and philosophies of de Sade, or on de Sade's life, or on some fictional notion of de Sade or his family.

Unsurprisingly, this categorization throws up a sector of cinema devoted in the majority – but by no means entirely – to films in the genres of horror and sex, both softcore and hardcore. But here you will also find films by respected *auteurs* such as Luis Buñuel and Pier Paolo Pasolini, or underground film-makers such as Japan's Takahiko Iimura and the German Aktionist Otto Muehl, and formats ranging from theatre adaptation to puppet animation.

Auteurs

Sadomania commences with an examination of two directors who have referenced de Sade time and again, directly and indirectly, throughout their corpus of work; the Spanish surrealist Luis Buñuel, and the Spanish exploitation director Jesus Franco, the two film-makers who have most overtly woven the philosophies and characters of the Marquis into the fabric of their texts, albeit in markedly different ways.

Continuing the juxtaposition between "art" and "cult", the book also includes Stephen Barber's examination of *Salò*, Pier Paolo Pasolini's notorious, terminal adaptation of de Sade's masterpiece *The 120 Days Of Sodom*, and concludes with a look at de Sade in that most shunned of all genres, hardcore pornography, as Xavier Mendik focuses on the specifically de Sade-related films of Italian director Joe D'Amato.

One other *auteur* who has, though without referencing de Sade directly, produced an undeniably sadean body of work is Japan's Koji Wakamatsu. Wakamatsu's most extreme films of sadean violence are *Embryo* (1964) and, in particular, his masterpiece *Violated Angels* (1966). Wakamatsu's frame of reference can perhaps be gauged by the *nom-de-plume* of his scriptwriter, Masao Adachi: "Marukido Sadao".

When Wakamatsu shot *Embryo*, his previous film, the voyeuristic *Secret Acts Within Four Walls* (1964) had been effectively suppressed by its producers; Wakamatsu quit in protest to start his own production company, and was quoted in the Western press as proclaiming: "For me, violence, the body and sex are an integral part of life"; as borne out by the film and its successors, this proved to be less an artistic defense than a genuine manifesto.

Palpably still enraged by the adverse reaction to *Secret Acts*, Wakamatsu throws into *Embryo* every sexual psychosis, cinematic gut-punch and accompanying outrage his revolutionary imagination can spew forth. The scenario of *Embryo* (aka *The Embryo Hunts In Secret*) is simple; a disturbed man imprisons his girlfriend in his flat and subjects her to days of sadistic torture. But this simplicity is belied by the film's complex execution, its restless experimentation and fathomless undercurrents of spiritual anguish. Wakamatsu's *Embryo* is film as a physical weapon, a razor through the eye of the beholder.

Legend has it that Wakamatsu, inflamed by the provocative 1966 news story of Chicago nurse-killer Richard Speck[11], conceived and executed his extraordinary film *Violated Angels* (released in 1967) within a week of hearing about it. *Violated Angels* opens with a series of still images, intercutting street scenes of the film's lead player, the actor/playwright Juro Kara, with images of nude women in provocative poses taken from commercial pornography. This establishes Kara's character as a disaffected individual with potentially unhealthy obsessions, an impression compounded by the first live-action scene, which

shows him at night, discharging a handgun into the ocean. The immediate, obvious associations of gun as phallus and sea as maternal are deliberate and sustained powerfully throughout the remainder of Wakamatsu's hour-long, sado-sexual death trip. Like the torturer in *Embryo*, this is a dangerous young man: mother-fixated, impotent, only able to express himself sexually through violence. A man who seemingly wants to fuck, kill, annihilate all women.

Violated Angels is a work of primal genius in which Wakamatsu reveals the ineluctable sexual pulse of the universe, and the cycles of birth, death, and rebirth that govern all matter. *Violated Angels* aligns this catamenial compulsion with the melancholy of the exposed embryo, the unbearable isolation in time and space that drives us to our daily rites of annihilation, and in doing so becomes perhaps the ultimate expression of sadean cinema as Wakamatsu evokes de Sade's credo of sexual violence, blasphemy, revolution, cosmic atavism and the annihilation of the nuclear family as encapsulated in his *Philosophy In The Boudoir* (1798), a polymorphous rite which ends with the mother – the eternal betrayer – being punished by having her vagina sewn shut (also denying re-entry to the sundered foetus)[12]. The sadean impulses which drive Wakamatsu's *Embryo* reach complete fruition in *Violated Angels*, an absolute indictment of the human condition expressed with perverse, poetic savagery.

Both these films by Wakamatsu were seen as extremely shocking in the West when first released, but much less so in Japan. As film titles like *Sadistic Song*, *Airline Stewardess Captured By Sex-Sadist*, *Sadistic Vampire* and *Sadistic Violence Against Ten Virgins* strongly imply, erotic cinema in Japan (known as "pink" cinema) has always been heavily inflected with themes and scenes of sadistic violence against women (and, much more rarely, against men by women). Yoshihiro Kawasaki's *Madamu Sado: Mesu Jigoku* (*Madame de Sade: She-Beast In Hell*, 1986) is typical fare; a minimal plot, with repetitive scenes of hardcore sado-masochism. Yumi ("M. de Sade") captures her former lover and his bride on their wedding day, and submits them to torture and sexual degradation in a basement dungeon. Interesting for its scenes of a female sadist who binds, buggers and tortures a male victim (an unusual reversal to the standard "pink movie" set-up of women being raped and tortured by men), but there is no direct connection to the Marquis' writings.

Very different from these films is *De Sade* (1962) by underground Tokyo director Takahiko Iimura, more known for his film *Ai* (*Love*, 1962). *De Sade* is a short (10 minutes) experimental film that utilizes 18th century lithographs to illustrate de Sade and *120 Days Of Sodom*, set to erotic whispers, contemporary pop music and Michaut's *Notre-Dame Mass*.

Film Adaptations

Adaptations of de Sade range from hardcore porn to black comedy, and come from all corners of the world. Most film adaptations of de Sade are of his major works: *Justine*, *Juliette*, *Philosophy In The Boudoir*, and *The 120 Days Of Sodom*. It is these four texts, bibles of pornographic atrocity all, which have, understandably, most inspired film-makers over the years. From de Sade's other literary works – of which there are quite a few, though all little-known – only a handful of films have ever sprung. These include: *Dialogue Between A Dying Man And A Priest* (Raymond Lefevre, 1965) from de Sade's short philosophical fiction; and the experimental *Eugenie de Franval* (Louis Skorecki, 1974) from de Sade's novel. *Eugenie de Franval* also served as inspiration – loosely – for two films by Jess Franco:

Eugénie (aka *De Sade 2000*, 1970); and a 1980 "remake", *Eugenie, Historia de una Perversion* (aka *Erotismo*) both of which also incorporate elements from de Sade's *Philosophy In The Boudoir*. *Eugénie* stars Soledad Miranda as Eugénie de Franval, a young girl drawn into a web of erotic cruelty by her stepfather. Together they plan to abduct and murder random victims, but the man's jealousy leads to tragedy. *Eugenie, Historia de una Perversion* features another sleazy couple who stalk, deflower and corrupt a teenage girl (the actress is rumoured to have been only fifteen) who likes to walk around nude and play with dolls. Lina Romay plays a submissive "dog".

"Philosophy In The Boudoir"

Once again, Jess Franco leads the way with films based on, or at least inspired by this, the most concise of de Sade's porno-erotic classics. *Eugenie, The Story Of Her Journey Into Perversion* (aka

De Sade 70, 1969) stars Christopher Lee as Dolmancé, leader of a sinister cult that preaches libertine values to its acolytes. One such couple decide to corrupt a young girl, Eugenie, played by Marie Lillejahl, and use her as sexual plaything. With nudity, softcore sex and some fairly tame whipping scenes. Franco also includes elements of lesbianism and incest, as well as his customary blurring of reality, and this is one of his better films production-wise.

Franco's *Plaisir A Trois* (aka *How To Seduce A Virgin*, 1973) was billed as a remake of *Eugenie...*, but differs even more from de Sade's original. The film features Alice Arno, Howard Vernon and Lina Romay in a tale of a wealthy family who kidnap, kill and collect the preserved bodies of beautiful young girls. A typical Franco movie with plenty of sadean touches, but little to do with its alleged source material. Trace elements of Sade's book may also be found in the Franco films *Sinfonia Erotica* (1979), *Gemidos de Placer* (1982), *Sexual Story Of O* (1984) and *Tender Flesh* (1998).

The other notable version of *Boudoir* aside from Franco's is that directed in 1970 by Jacques Scandelari, a film also known in English as *Beyond Love and Evil.* In Scandelari's version, a young man accompanies his fiancee to a mansion which turns out to be the site of all manner of ongoing sexual debauchery. Wall-wall nudity, whippings, softcore sex, psychedelic orgies whose participants have painted faces, rape, miscegeny, homosexuality and lesbianism, and even a woman who likes to masturbate with live squid, all feature in this bizarre "pop art" sexual free-for-all.

One other direct version of *Philosophy In The Boudoir* is Tony Guzman's *Philosophy In The Bedroom* (USA, 1995). Filmed in black-and-white, this is a mediocre, somewhat camp exposition of de Sade.

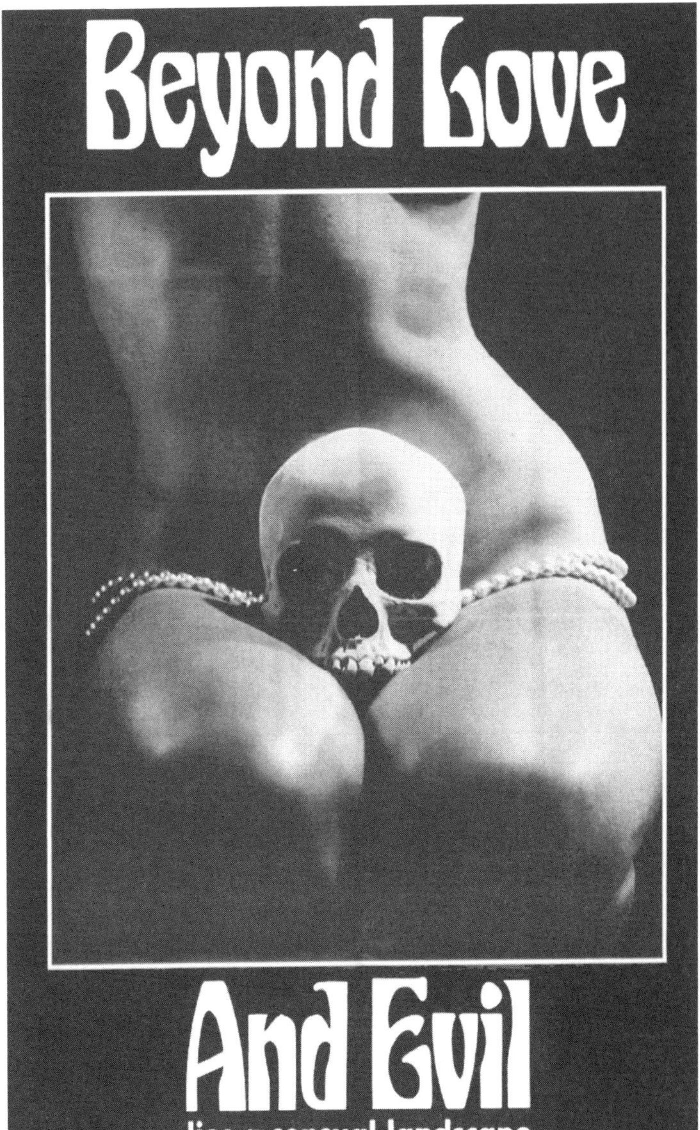
Beyond Love
And Evil
lies a sensual landscape

Finally, it took intrepid New York "transgressive" filmmaker Richard Kern to emulate one of the book's more shocking incidents – when Eugenie stitches up her mother's vagina – for real, when he filmed actress Kembra Pfhaler having her own vagina stitched shut in his short movie *The Sewing Circle* (1992).

"Justine" and "Juliette"

These two huge volumes are the most popular, and most filmed, of de Sade's works. And, as with the name of de Sade himself, Justine has also been a name much used in porno films to garner interest by association; for example, *Justine: The Erotic Excitement of Evil* (1967); *Hot Nights Of Justine* (1976); Roberta Findlay's *Justine – A Matter Of Innocence* (1980) – a regular nympho-porn film set in modern-day America; *The Spectre Of Justine* (1986); *Justine* (1992), an X-rated incest fantasy; and a whole series of "Justine" films from France including *Justine: Exotic Liaisons* (1995), *Justine: Wild Nights* (1995), and *Justine: In The Heat Of Passion* (1996). And finally – *Virgin Kink #6* (USA, 1998) starred not only Jamie Gillis but also a pair of sado-maso-porno twins by the names of Juliette and Justine Réage.

More relevant versions of de Sade's twin pornographic epics have been made in many different countries – including Great Britain, Spain, France, Scandinavia, and Japan.

Two Japanese films of interest here are: *Onna Jigoku: Mori Wa Nureta* (*Woman In Hell: Wet Forest* (Tatsumi Kumashiro, 1973) based on a part of de Sade's *Justine*, and Akio Jissoji's *Akutoku No Sakae* (*Prosperities Of Vice*, 1988, based on de Sade's *Juliette). Woman In Hell: Wet Forest* is a Nikkatsu production, a prime example of the "roman porn" genre which that company pioneered in the 1970s. Roman porn films were notable for their high production values, gorgeous leading ladies and skilled direction; Kumashiro himself was one of Nikkatsu's leading film-makers, sometimes referred to as the "king of roman porn", and his other genre classics included *Black Rose Rising* (1975) and *Woman With Red Hair* (1979). In *Wet Forest*, Sachiko, a young runaway girl is picked up by Yoko, an elegant woman who takes her to live in secluded, candlelit country mansion. Once there she finds herself in the company of other girls and male "guests" who are held captive in cages and subjected to rape, torture and whippings at the hands of Ryunosuke-san, the master of the house. This short (65 minutes) film is bleak, dark and claustrophobic and in its conflation of sex and death as extreme as anything made by Wakamatsu.

The film's central sequence is a sadistic sexual orgy that climaxes in bloody slaughter. The orgy involves Yoko and Ryunosuke, Sachiko, two other slave girls and two male captives. After the two males are simultaneously fellated and masturbated by Yoko, one of them fucks her whilst the other rapes one of the girls. At this point Ryunosuke enters the action, first whipping the men and then sodomizing each in turn, even as they fuck the women. After more interactions he then pulls a gun and shoots one of the men point-blank in the head; blood drenches the girl beneath. Yoko then shoots the man who is fucking her, laughing as his blood jets out. The scene ends with an array of blood-soaked girls, dead bodies and sexually sated sadists sprawled across one of the beds.

After this sexual massacre, the mens' nude corpses are laid out across the dining-table while Sachiko and the killer couple eat dinner, before burying the bodies in the cellar.

While the sex in *Wet Forest* is never explicit – Japanese porn is always genitally censored[13] – Kumashiro's film remains a highly disturbing sadean work that purveys an aura of rank, lethal sexual perversion underpinned by an annihilatory philosophy to unnerving effect.

Akio Jissoji's *Prosperities Of Vice* is a slow-paced and overly stagey meditation on de Sade's *Juliette*, concerning the machinations of a debauched and voyeuristic aristocrat who stages a play based on the epic novel in which his wife takes the title role. Lacking in sex for such a project, this is a sophisticated but ultimately boring exercise, which never really betters its bizarre opening sequence of strawberries erupting from the smouldering abdomen of a Bellmeresque doll, intercut with close-ups of pages from early French illustrated editions of de Sade. Jissoji followed up a year later with *Ijmete Kudasai Henrietta* (*Please Abuse Me, Henrietta* aka *De Sade's Henrietta* aka *Justine, Disciple Of De Sade*, 1989), inspired by de Sade's short story "Miss Henrietta Stralson"; a young widow is forced to take up prostitution to pay off family debts, and finds herself enmeshed in the bleak world of sado-masochism.

Swedish hardcore director Mac Ahlberg directed his *Justine and Juliette* in 1975, in which the two sisters make their way in the world through different ways – Justine pious but impoverished, Juliette a money-grabbing prostitute who endlessly resells her faked virginity. With plenty and nudity plus hardcore sex scenes (involving Harry Reems), but little in the way of sadean cruelty, this modern-day rendition of the two sisters is ultimately an average, if well-photographed, porno movie with an edge of farce.

From the UK came Chris Boger's *Cruel Passion* (1977), a predictably tame version of *Justine* starring American actress Koo Stark. Lesbian nun scenes add some interest, but overall there is very little in the way of nudity, sex or sadism to enliven this period adaptation.

Lorenzo Sabatini's *Juliette de Sade* (1969) was an Italian-Swedish production in which Juliette leaves her sequestered convent life and heads to Rome, where she meets a libertine disciple of de Sade. At first intrigued, she soon becomes disgusted by the life of dissolution which he plans for her.

From France, Roger Vadim's *Vice and Virtue* (1963) was an early film to incorporate the two sisters into a plot involving fascism (in this case, Nazis), thus anticipating the theme of Pasolini's later *Salo*. But despite using talented actresses Catherine Deneuve and Anne Giradot, Vadim's rather tame vision is light-hearted by comparison, and distinctly void of sexual excitement. Also from France is Claude Pierson's *Justine de Sade* (1972), probably the best of all the screen versions. Alice Arno plays Justine, an innocent young girl who undergoes a lengthy series of tortures, rapes and beatings at the hands of monks and

other supposed authority figures. Far more sadean in cruelty than its peers, the film also shows an inventiveness distinctly lacking in the others. *Justine de Sade* is a non-stop series of vivid, sometimes disturbing sexual debauches, with Arno displaying every inch of her naked body to salacious effect.

"120 Days of Sodom"

The most (in)famous of all adaptations of this (or any) book by de Sade remains Pasolini's monumental *Salò* (see Chapter III), while the most hardcore is Joe D'Amato's less faithful *120 Days Of The Anal* aka *Anal Palace* (see Chapter IV). The most notable version apart from these is Marco Ferreri's Buñuelian black comedy *La Grande Bouffe* (aka *Blow-Out*, 1973), which modifies the plot somewhat in that the four (modern-day) "libertines" have now decided to eat themselves to death in an orgy of unbridled gluttony. The four, played by noted European actors Marcello Mastroianni, Ugo Tognazzi, Michel Piccoli and Philippe Noiret, hole themselves up in a mansion, accompanied by prostitutes, and start their bizarre suicide ritual. Sex, perversion, scatology, aberrant philosophy and finally death are the elements that combine to make this a sadean film of the highest order.

The influence of de Sade, and *120 Days Of Sodom* in particular, can be also seen in the film work of the Vienna Aktionist Otto Muehl. Muehl's series of short "Aktion scripts" from 1964 read very much like the appreviated atrocities listed by de Sade in the final sections of that book; for example: "a*n 80-year-old grandmother is tied to an easy chair 13 m away from the lens of a film projector; an experimental film (16 mm) prepared with ddt e605 blue vitriol poisoned wheat and fly agaric powder is projected on to the wrinkled old hag; the old grandmother passes away in the poisoned flickering of the experimental film*" (Otto Muehl, *Action Script XXVIII*). The coprophagic excremental inferno of *120 Days* was recreated in Muehl's *Scheisskerl* of 1969. In *Scheisskerl*, actress Hanel Koeck administers an enema to another woman, who shits copiously over Muehl's prone body; Koeck then proceeds to smear the hot shit all over his body, masturbate him, and finally fellate him before the first woman sits astride him and guides his erect cock into her filthy wet anus. Another Muehl film of that year, *O Sensibility!*, also recalls de Sade's "bestiality" manias[14]. In this film, a girl "makes love" to a live goose. Finally the goose is decapitated and its blood-spurting neck-stump inserted into her vagina. Muehl capped off this trilogy of cinematic blasphemies with *Sodoma* (1970) As the title implies, this film strongly echoes de Sade's *120 Days* with its relentless scenes of buggery, fucking, sucking, pissing, the tying up and/or

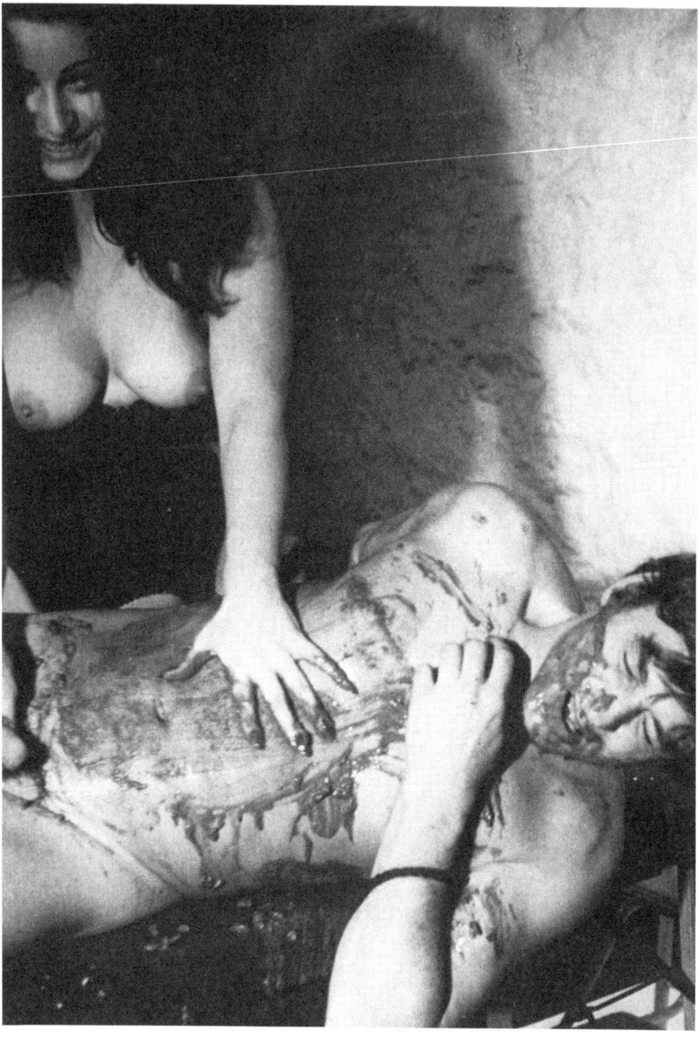

hanging up of the participants, the introduction of liquids and objects into vaginas and anuses, and mass orgiastic abandon.

"Biographical" Films

Most biographical films about de Sade are at least partly fictionalized, whilst others veer into the realms of the completely fantastic. The first substantial screen portrayal of the Marquis de Sade was by Patrick Magee in Peter Brook's *The Marat/Sade* of 1967, a film of a play and a play within a film, showing the inmates of Charenton asylum performing a theatrical piece written for them by de Sade – hence the film's full title, *The Persecution and Assassination of Jean-Paul Marat as Performed by the Inmates of the Asylum of Charenton Under the Direction of the Marquis de Sade.* As the play progresses, the "actors" gradually lose control and, spurred on by the anti-authoritarian Marquis, plunge the whole madhouse into violent chaos. Magee gives a customarily powerful performance, seething with both subversion and perversion, and Brook transcends the film's stage origins by his

lucid and mobile camera-work. Inspired by Antonin Artaud's Theatre of Cruelty, Peter Weiss's original play was also produced for television in Finland (*Jean-Paul Marat förföljd och mördad så som det framställs av patienterna på hospitalet Charenton under ledning av herr de Sade*) that same year.

The Marat/Sade was followed in the US by two very contrasting efforts: Richard Hilliard's *I, Marquis de Sade* (1967) is an inconsequential low-budget, softcore porn romp featuring Russ Meyer starlet Babette Bardot; this was followed by the first major big screen biography of de Sade, Cy Endfield's *De Sade* (1969), a fairly lavish Hollywood production starring Keir Dullea and John Huston[15]. Intelligently scripted by Richard Matheson, the film uses flashbacks and theatrical framing devices as the Marquis looks back on his life and crimes. Some nudity and intimations of sadism, but overall this is a fairly safe, mainstream production.

Meanwhile, Swedish porn director Mac Ahlberg came up with the unusual Danish co-production *Jeg-en-Marki* (1967, co-directed by Peer Guldbrandsen), which is an attempt to see how de Sade might fare in modern times. An accountant suffering from acute depression due to financial worries decides to make a last desperate change in his life, and takes on the name – soon followed by the persona – of M.D.E. Sade. He begins stealing money from his clients and living up to his new aristocratic identity, "becoming" the reincarnation of de Sade. People start to treat him with respect, and at the mere mention of his name, even highly respectable members of the upper class Scandinavian society are triggered into the wildest, most erotic, sadistic and masochistic fantasies imaginable. Known in English as *The Reluctant Sadist*.

Definitely the most bizarre de Sade "biopic" of them all must be Henri Xhonneux's *Marquis* (1989), co-scripted by former

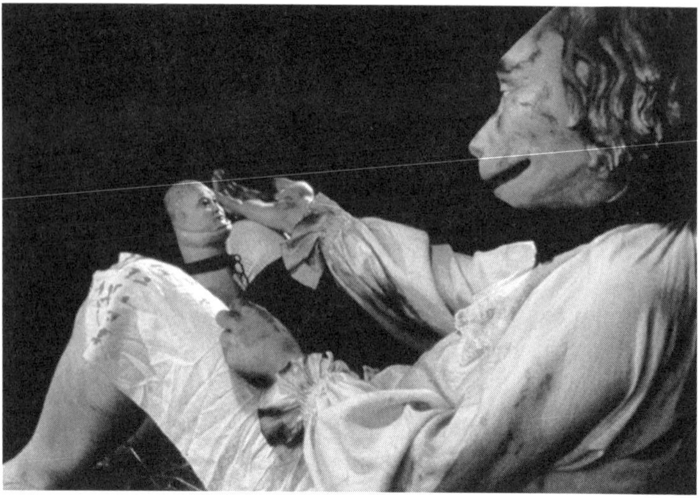

Panic Movement member Roland Topor. The film depicts various scenes from both de Sade's books and from his life in the Bastille, and all the characters are represented by anthropomorphic animals, played by actors with garish masks. There are also sequences of stop-motion animation – most notably when the Marquis (a dog) engages in discussions with his own penis, which has its own face and voice. Other grotesque sequences include the rape of a cow-woman with blood-spurting udders, a spider turning into eight female crotches, and a rat-man sodomised by a lobster tail. Like an obscene surrealist reverie, *Marquis* is a true missive from the nightside of the imagination, and as such stands as a rare fitting tribute to its subject.

Other more recent and conventional biopix have included Gwyneth Gibby's *Dark Prince* (1996), Philip Kaufman's *Quills* (2000), and Benoît Jacquot's *Sade* (2000). Of these, *Quills* is by far the most interesting. Set, like the earlier *Marat/Sade*, in Charenton asylum, the film details both de Sade's clashes with authority as he stages more and more subversive theatrical productions for the inmates, and also the final love/sex affair of his life, conducted with a 13-year-old serving girl. Finally, *Quills* reduces de Sade's existence to a monomaniacal obsession with the written word and his refusal to be silenced; incarcerated without access to pens or paper, he continues to write in his own blood and faeces, on every available surface. His final punishment is to have his tongue cut out, in the film's melodramatic, gore-splattered Grand Guignol highlight.

Coda: Sado-Masochism

The popular notion that "every masochist needs a sadist" is not strictly true, however the two psychosexual complexes are so closely linked that it seems impossible to mention one without the other. With hundreds, even thousands of films featuring sado-masochistic activities, it may be expedient here to keep with the literary theme of this study by just looking at films which have been directly based on or inspired by the three major written works of masochism: *Venus In Furs* by Sacher-Masoch (the book and author which gave us the term "masochism"); *The Story Of O* by Pauline Réage; and *The Image* by Jean de Berg.

Of four films bearing the title *Venus In Furs*, two are only slightly, if at all, related to the book in terms of story or content. Joseph Marzano's version of 1967 is a strange extended sexual fantasy, while Jess Franco's version (1969) is an equally bizarre oneiric meditation on sex, death and identity [see Chapter II]. The two films which are most faithful to the original book are by Massimo Dallamano (1969) and Victor Nieuwenhuijs and Maartje Seyferth (1994). Neither is a classic. Dallamano's version updates the story to the 1960s and features Laura Antonelli in many nude scenes as the girl whose lover insists she beat him and cheat on

him to give him perverse pleasure. Nieuwenhuijs and Seyferth's interpretation is shot in black-and-white and is very much an "art" film, with lingering long shots and little dialogue. Although there are plenty of nude scenes to catch the eye, it appears to be more about composition than psychological motivation.

Underground film-maker Kenneth Anger's attempted version of *The Story Of O*, commenced in 1961, was regrettably aborted when it turned out that money given to him by the boyfriend of the girl playing "O" was part of ransom paid out to kidnappers of Eric Peugeot, heir to the French automobile empire. It also transpired that the girl was the daughter of a priest, and when her parents heard about the film they immediately forbade her further participation. All that remains are a few intriguing still photos (although legend has it that the footage Anger shot is still hidden away somewhere – perhaps buried – in France). Which leaves two existing adaptations – one official, one not.

In 1975 Gerard Damiano, director of *Deep Throat* and probably the most notorious of all hardcore porn directors, decided to film a version of *The Story Of O*. Not bothering to secure permission, Damiano instead constructed his own script based on the book, and titled it *Story Of Joanna*. The film stars Terri Hall, Jamie Gillis and Zebedy Colt in a dark story about a dying libertine who is training his submissive female slave to shoot him as an act of mercy. She eventually does so after being released from servitude, and takes possession of his old dark mansion. With naked dancing, sex dreams, philosophies of pain and degradation, group sex, whippings, lesbian and homosexual scenes, various blow-jobs (including male on male), and some extraordinary close-up shots of oral sex, *Story Of Joanna* is one of Damiano's best hardcore features.

(Another porn film of the same year, *Journey Of O*, bears scant relationship to the novel and concerns a "urine-fixated" girl, Ophelia (played by Serena), being sent to a clinic for "aversion" treatment – which involves being abused by several men.)

Also in 1975 came the 'official" version of *The Story Of O*, directed by Just Jaekin and starring Udo Kier as René and Anthony Steel as Sir Stephen. O is played by Corinne Clery. This version of *O* is marked by its glossy, softcore fashion-shoot style which somewhat overwhelms the erotic charge generated in some

otherwise potent scenes of nudity, flagellation, branding, lesbianism and various acts of sexual intercourse. Jaekin's film nonetheless retains the core of the original novel and has stood the test of time as that relatively rare commodity, an "intelligent" adult movie.

The Fruits Of Passion: The Return Of O appeared in 1981, and was directed by Japanese film-maker Shuji Terayama, better known for underground films such as *Emperor Tomato Ketchup* (1970), with its scenes of sex between a nine-year-old boy and two women. His unofficial sequel to *O* stars Klaus Kinski as Sir Stephen and also features Isabelle Illiers as O. With its ad-line promising "the excruciating pain of endless pleasure", *The Fruits Of Passion* is set in 1920s Hong Kong and plays like an opiated fugue, with some explicit sex scenes, mild bondage, and murder.

To date there has only been one cinematic version of *The Image: The Punishment Of Anne* (1975), directed by legendary soft- and hard-core porn director Radley Metzger. Metzger's sex films are renowned for their elegance and art, and *The Punishment Of Anne* is no exception; it may, indeed, be his masterpiece. It closely follows the chapters of the original book, in which Anne is the "property" of her mistress Claire. There is little hardcore sex, but some explicit shots of pissing, inserting grapes into the vagina, and other fetishistic detail. Erotic photos, bondage, SM masks and whips, hot needles, chains, and a gothic torture chamber complete the overall picture of sexual/psychological dominance and submission in this most elegant of literary adaptations, deservedly regarded as a classic.

Notes

1. De Sade's evil reputation was sealed – at least in England – when copies of his books were found, alongside others by and about Adolf Hitler, in the collection of child killer Ian Brady in the early 60s.

2. *Petit maison* was the term used to describe an aristocrat's second home, usually located in a suburban or semi-rural area, where he could indulge in orgiastic pursuits away from the public eye.

3. Restif de la Bretonne (1734–1806) was a man of letters who had an intense rivalry with the Marquis de Sade. He even tried to compete with de Sade in terms of pornography, producing in 1798 his magnum opus *The Anti-Justine*, a pornographic novelization of Restif's own life and sexual debauches, which the author tried to defend "morally" by declaring his book to be an "antidote" to the supposed poison of de Sade; yet whilst the book opens with a spurious warning to women against cruelty, it soon develops into a monumental odyssey of sexual depravity which often rivals de Sade in its relentless explicitness.

4. "[...] A definition of sadism that will include all forms of passive and active algolagnia, zoöphilia, necrophilia, symbolic algolagnia, etc., is essential. It should be remembered that since actual and ideal destructive processes in nature appear as causes of sexual excitation and satisfaction, such as eruptions, storms, fires, murders, etc., sadism must be defined in the following way. Sadism is the purposively sought or accidentally presented connection of sexual excitation and pleasure with the actual or also only symbolic (ideal or illusory) occurrences of strange and terrifying events, destructive processes and actions, which threaten or destroy life, health and property of men or other living beings whereby the person receiving sexual pleasure from such events may be the originator or spectator, voluntary or involuntary. We believe that this definition covers all cases of sadism, including word-sadism, torture, forms of rape, etc" –Iwan Bloch, *De Sade: Life And Works*.

5. De Sade has also appeared as a character in several other minor horror features, including: *Waxwork* (1988), *Exotic House Of Wax* (1996), *Dead 2: The Skull Of Pain* (1997), and *Go To Hell* (1999). Perhaps the earliest horror reference to the Marquis came in Pat Boyette's *Dungeon Of Harrow* (1962), in which one Count Lorente de Sade, an evil sadist, presides over a gloomy waterfront castle with his wife, the Countess.

6. This trick is not exclusive to sleaze-pedlars. Situationist Guy Debord's experimental *Hurlements En Faveur de Sade* (*Howlings In Favour Of de Sade*, 1952) has nothing to do with de Sade save for its title.

7. *Daughters Of Discipline*, for example, is described in the Avon catalog as follows: *"CJ Laing receives the death card (black skull and crossbones), foreboding symbol of her*

forthcoming sacrifice. Now she masturbates, reminiscing upon her initiation into the death cult. Two men in black leather masks whip her bloody. Filthy talk and graphic cum-shots follow. Later, CJ is strapped into a chair with an electrified dildo up her cunt. More foul fucking primes her for the inevitable death ritual".

8. In 1986, the Meese Commission against pornography cited Prince's films as the most rank, foul and violent examples of pornography in the USA.

9. The two hardcore movies which are probably most closely connected to De Sade are actually Joe D'Amato's *Marquis de Sade* and *120 Days Of The Anal* (see chapter IV).

10. *Olga's House Of Shame* (1964), *Olga's Girls* (1964), *Madame Olga's Massage Parlor* (1965), and *Olga's Dance Hall Girls* (1966).

11. Around midnight on July 13, 1966, Corazon Amurao, a young nurse of Filipino origin, heard someone knocking on the door of her Chicago dormitory. She opened up sleepily, and a young pock-marked man strongly smelling of alcohol violently entered the house. It was 25-year-old Richard Speck, a man whose life had been determined by misogyny and sexual offences. Speck threatened the young female residents with a gun, tied them, and finally dragged one after the other into an adjoining room. Muffled screams emanated as the deranged intruder brutally strangled or stabbed his helpless victims. One of the nurses seemed to remind him of his hated ex-wife (she was 15 when they married); he raped her both vaginally and anally before mutilating her. All in all, the violator claimed the lives of eight girls. Corazon Amurao alone survived the massacre hidden under a bed, and identified Speck later, above all because of the distinctive tattoo on his arm – "Born to raise Hell". In the course of their investigation the police began to suspect that Richard Speck, the nurse-killer of Chicago, was also responsible for a series of still unsolved sex murders in the area of the Great Lakes. He had, after all, been there at the time of the crimes. The tattooed "rockabilly-killer" (complete with Elvis quiff and leather jacket) was duly sentenced to multiple imprisonment for life – 600 years– without remission.

12. De Sade took these codes to their murderous conclusion in *The 120 Days Of Sodom*, in which his libertines devise endless ways to fornicate with and then butcher mothers, daughters, prostitutes, pregnant women and little girls alike.

13. In fact Kumashiro, in *Wet Forest*, makes something of a protest against this by using vastly over-sized black censor boxes during the sex scenes. The effect is to heighten the film's edgy feel, which is also reflected in its sudden jumps from bright colour to blue-tint and occasional use of fractive frame-editing.

14. For example: *"30. This libertine fucks a turkey whose head is gripped between the thighs of a nude, prostrate girl, so it appears he is buggering her. As he pumps away his valet sodomizes him without mercy, and at the moment he ejaculates, the girl slits the turkey's throat. ... 33. He wishes to see a woman come to orgasm as a dog licks out her*

cunt; the very moment she comes, he blows the dog's head off with a pistol. The woman is unharmed. 34. He buggers a swan after coining a Host up its anus, and throttles it to death as he sprays out his ball-juice." From *120 Days of Sodom* (Solar Books, 2008).

15. Several other de Sade biopix have been announced over the years, but never came to fruition; these include a 1971 project by Alain Resnais, in which de Sade was due to be played by Dirk Bogarde, and another in 1993 by Paul Verhoeven, for which Jack Nicholson and Gérard Depardieu were amongst the contenders to play the Marquis.

I
LUIS BUÑUEL: THE FIRST SADIST

Luis Buñuel (1900-1983), one of the most original film-makers of all time, had a lifelong obsession with the works of the Marquis de Sade which continually informed, to varying degrees, the texts of his films. In his autobiography *My Last Sigh*, Buñuel tells us: "I was about twenty-five when I read *120 Days Of Sodom* for the first time, and I must admit I found it far more shocking than Darwin. One day, when I was visiting Roland Tual, I saw a priceless copy in his library that had originally belonged to Marcel Proust. Despite its rarity, Tual lent it to me. It was a revelation. Up until then, I'd heard nothing of de Sade, although the professors at the University of Madrid prided themselves on the fact that they never hid anything from their students... ...so how was it that I knew nothing about this systematic and magisterial exploration of society, this proposal for such a sweeping annihilation of culture? When I could bring myself to admit that the university had lied, I found that next to de Sade, all other masterpieces paled."

In the very first moments of his very first film, *Un Chien Andalou* (1929, co-made with Salvador Dali), Buñuel set the tone for the rest of his career and produced perhaps the cinema's first authentic moment of sadean violence. The film opens with the notorious sequence of a man, played by Buñuel himself, slitting open a women's eye with a cut-throat razor. Shot in graphic close-

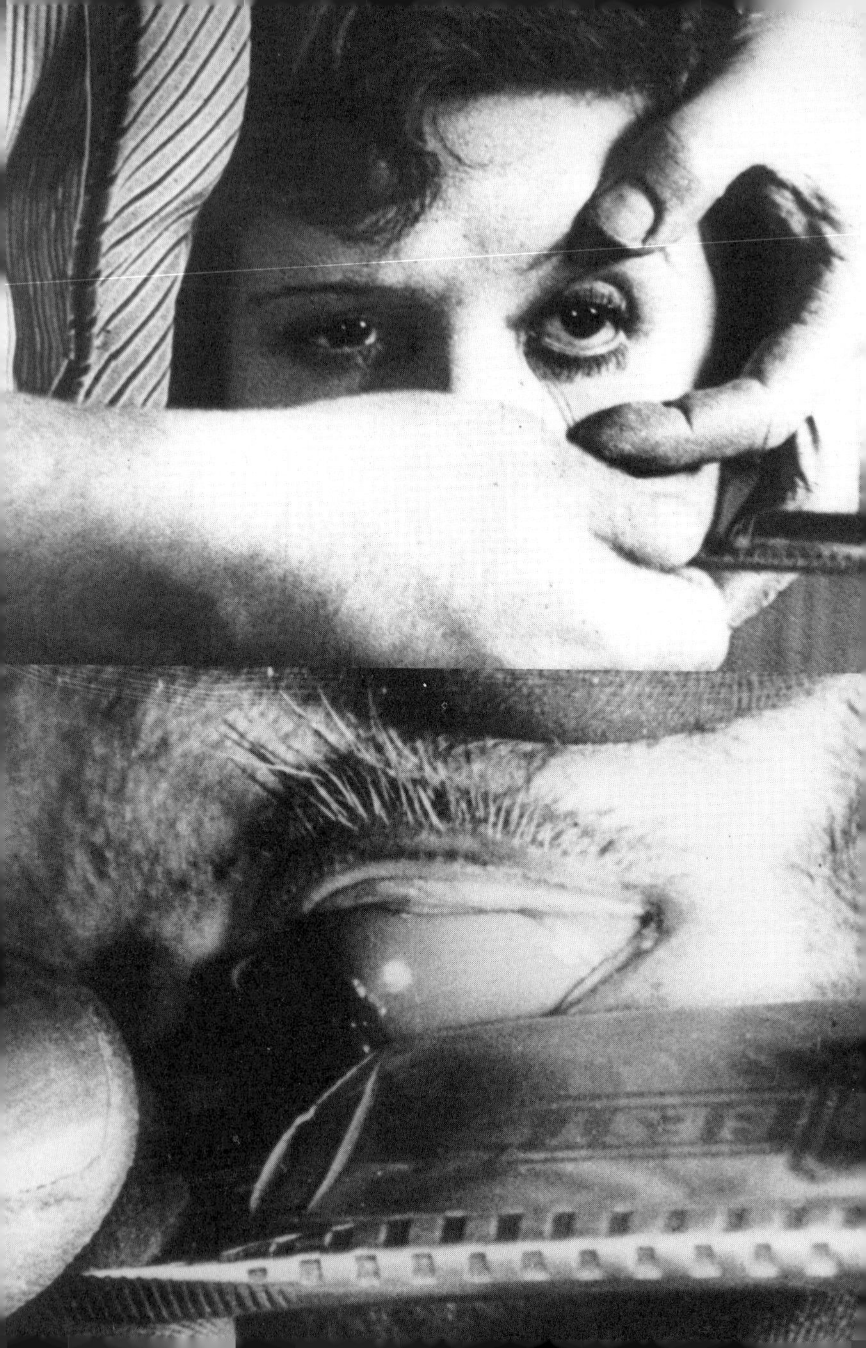

up (using a dead animal's eye) this scene retains its convulsive power decades later. The casual act of mutilation, seemingly enacted with the woman's consent and set against 'romantic" shots of a full moon, suggests the most terrible of complicit and destructive sexual perversions.

But it was in his next film, *L'Age d'Or* (1930) that Buñuel would become the first film-maker to directly re-enact scenes from one of de Sade's works – in this case, *120 Days Of Sodom.* The sequence in question comes at the end of the hour-long film, and depicts the four libertines of de Sade's novel at the end of their murderous debauches. The scenes are described in Buñuel's original script as follows:

"237... Vertical panorama rising until it discloses a mountain, abrupt and enormous, covered with snow. At the edge of a precipice the threatening silhouette of a medieval chateau rears up.

"A long shot of the chateau.

"A long shot of the front with its gate closed.

"Subtitle (in double exposure with falling feathers). 'AT THE EXACT MOMENT WHEN THESE FEATHERS, TORN OUT BY HIS FURIOUS HANDS, COVERED THE EARTH AT THE BASE OF THE WINDOW – AT THAT MOMENT, WE SAY, BUT FAR AWAY, THE SURVIVORS OF THE CHATEAU DE SELLINY WERE SETTING OFF TO RETURN TO PARIS TO CELEBRATE THE MOST BRUTAL OF ORGIES, THEY HAD BEEN LOCKED UP, 120 DAYS PREVIOUSLY, THESE FOUR ABSOLUTE, UNMISTAKABLE SCOUNDRELS, WHO HAVE NO GOD BUT THEIR LUST, NO LAW BUT THEIR DEPRAVITY, NO BRAKE BUT THEIR DEBAUCHERY, LIBERTINES WITHOUT GOD, WITHOUT PRINCIPLES, WITHOUT RELIGION, THE LEAST CRIMINAL OF THEM

DEFILED BY MORE WICKEDNESS THAN YOU COULD POSSIBLY ENUMERATE, IN WHOSE EYES THE LIFE OF A WOMAN – WHAT AM I SAYING, ONE WOMAN, ALL THE WOMEN ON THE FACE OF THE EARTH – IS AS TRIVIAL A THING AS SWATTING A FLY. THEY BROUGHT WITH THEM INTO THE CHATEAU, SOLELY TO SERVE THEIR FILTHY DESIGNS, EIGHT MARVELOUS GIRLS, EIGHT MAGNIFICENT TEENAGERS, AND, SO THAT THEIR IMAGINATION (ALREADY CORRUPTED BY EXCESS) SHOULD BE CONTINUALLY EXCITED, THEY LIKEWISE BROUGHT ALONG FOUR DEPRAVED WOMEN WHO UNCEASINGLY FED THE CRIMINAL SENSUALITY OF THE FOUR MONSTERS WITH THEIR STORIES. HERE NOW LEAVING THE CHATEAU DE SELLINY ARE THE SURVIVORS OF THESE CRIMINAL ORGIES; THE FOUR ORGANIZERS AND LEADERS: THE DUC DE BLANGIS

"238. Close-up of the portal, which opens very slowly as if the rust of its hinges were holding it back. The haloed head of a man appeared, with beard and mustache, dressed in the manner of Hebrews of the first century of our era.

"239. A slightly longer shot to allow a full-length view of the Duc de Blangis. His eyes, half-closed after the great prison, are dazzled by the snow-glare. He looks behind him to see if anyone is following, and proceeds forward.

"Subtitle: PRESIDENT CURVAL AND FINANCIER DURCET

"One after the other, they come out, one dressed in the Oriental manner of fourth century B.C., the other like an ordinary Arab (sixth century A.D.). Both, after noting the course taken by the leader go in that direction.

"Subtitle: THE REMAINING ONE OF THE FOUR: THE BISHOP OF K

"The last character comes limping out, dressed like a 16th century priest. He heads in the same direction as the others. All should come out and walk rapidly.

"240. Background shot of the first character near a snow-covered rock, in the attitude of someone waiting for another, in order to start out at once. The others come into the shot and without saying a word go close to the first, similarly waiting for the remaining one.

"241. Long shot of the portal which has remained ajar. For a while, the portal by itself.

"A little girl of about 13, on the doorstep, terrorized, dressed in a big chemise, holding her bosom with one of her hands at the place corresponding to one of her breasts, covered with bloodstains.

"242. She has fallen exhausted on the very threshold; the

last of the characters re-enters the scene and, taking the little girl in his arms, carries her into the chateau. Pause, during which nothing unusual occurs, except a great, terrifying scream from the interior; a few moments later, the same character, impassive, goes to join the rest, accordingly leaving the scene.

"243. A deep white snow... Lashed by the snow and the wind, moving one after the other at the right of the scene, coming up to a long shot (let the actors walk up an inclined ramp), are the four impassive characters.

"From above – a snow-covered cross covered with locks of women's hair, cruelly blown about by the wind whitened with snow."

The scenes in the final film differ somewhat – the subtitles are shorter, the scene less cut-up; only the Duc de Blangis is dressed as a "Hebrew", the others in 18th century garb; it is Blangis who finally finishes off the little girl – but Buñuel's intent remains clear. Lust-murder, blasphemy, and a jarring tribute to his most revered author. His conflation of Christ with Blangis, de Sade's sexually-driven serial killer, remains a gesture of severe provocation. With *L'Age d'Or*, he had produced the first ever landmark of Sadean cinema.

Buñuel's fliratation with de Sade continued throughout the subsequent decades. As well as a general reverence to de Sade's tenets, there are also more specific instances. For example, the protagonist of *El* resolves to sew up his wife's vagina, just as Eugénie does to her mother in de Sade's *Philosophy In The Boudoir*. Buñuel shows us the sinister tools that will be needed for the job – needle, thread, disinfectant, cotton wool. This was also referenced on the poster art for Buñuel's later *That Discreet Object Of Desire* (1977) which showed a pair of female lips stitched together.

In Buñuel's *La Voie Lactée* (aka *The Milky Way*, 1969), de Sade is actually portrayed by Michel Piccoli, and the script quotes from the Marquis liberally. *The Milky Way* is the tale of two tramps on a pilgrimage. As their journey progresses they encounter different characters from varying periods of history, all engaged in theological debate or indulging in religious absurdities. These include the Marquis de Sade who is seen in a dungeon, delivering an atheistic, anti-Christian rant to a girl in chains. De Sade's tirade ends with the succinct: "If your God exists, how I hate him!". Although nearly all Buñuel's films feature scenes of mental or physical cruelty, mutilation, sexual perversion, or blasphemy which could all be referenced back to de Sade, *The Milky Way* is perhaps the film which, after *L'Age D'Or*, most specifically references the Marquis both visually and in philosophical terms, albeit in this one relatively short sequence.

II
JESUS FRANCO: A SADEAN AUTEUR

1. Perverse Bodies, Profane Texts

"Sexual compulsions are part of the tragic limited fallible condition of man... doomed to endless repetitions that can never satisfy the ideal images of the spirit. There is nothing that reminds man of his precarious metaphysical situation than sex and it is not surprising that 'death' 'dying' and 'little death' should be words for orgasm both in English and in other European languages." –Maurice Charney, *Sexual Fiction.*

According to Maurice Charney, the connection between sexuality and death evident in a distinct tradition in European philosophy can be traced from the work of the Marquis de Sade to the later theorists such as Freud. In his formulation of the concept of the "death drive"[1], Freud retraces the connections between an excess of sexuality and annihilation identified in Sade's works such as *120 Days Of Sodom* (1785), *Justine* (1791), *Juliette* (1797) and *Philosophy In The Boudoir* (1795).

According to Freud's analysis, the unrepressed tensions which dominate infantile sexuality re-emerge in later life to retard sexual fulfilment and the secure construction of gender identity. This obsession with the traumas of infancy functions through a form of 'compulsive repetition'. This conflates images of sexual pleasure with those of death or impending mutilation which the sufferer continually fears. (Its effect was seen in Freud's patients such as the 'Wolf Man', who found his adult sexuality dominated by repeated and revised scenes of his discovery of a violent act of parental coitus during childhood)[2].

What this close connection between Sade and Freud reveals, is both the construction of human subjectivity through excessive sexual drives as well as the direction of these forms of gratification towards scenarios of annihilation and chaos. In this respect, they provide a useful template to consider the cinematic interests that have marked the phenomenal output of the Spanish fantasy director Jesus Franco. Arguably Franco's interests reflect his self-confessed interest with de Sade and the reformulation of his ideas in both European philosophy and aesthetics[3].

The importance of Sade's work extends beyond Franco's literal interpretation of his writings in films such as *Justine* (1968), in a systematic combination of images of sexuality, torture and death with an equally chaotic film style that has often bemused his admirers and detractors alike. What I shall argue is that it is not only the uncompromising content of Franco's work which warrants his definition as a sadean director, but also the preoccupation with generic deviation and narrative repetition which mark this influence on his film style. For instance, although Franco's work has varied in content and spanned genres as diverse as horror, pornography, action adventure and historical drama, all – from *Lustful Amazons* to *Lorna, The Exorcist* – share the preoccupation with the sexuality and death that Charney argues defines Sade's interests. The close connection between these physiological states is perfectly defined by two of his most controversial 1970s productions: *The Female Vampire* (1973) and *Doriana Gray* (1975).

In *The Female Vampire* (aka *The Bare-Breasted Countess*), Franco's long time partner and filmic collaborator Lina Romay is cast as the vampire Irina Karlstein who seduces a series of male and female partners before killing them at the point of sexual climax. In a marked departure from established cinematic traditions of the vampire, the source of Irina's oral gratifications is the genitals rather than the necks of potential victims. Indeed, the film reiterates its basis in writings such as *120 Days Of Sodom* via its staging of a sado-masochistic stage act which Irene visits. The construction of the sexual act as a site of both punishment and public consumption (evident in this scene and in many other Franco films)[4] confirms Charney's conclusion that in Sade, sexual pleasure is not only equated with annihilation but replaced by principles of pain and oppression.

If the heroine's obsession underscores *The Female Vampire*'s examination of the links between orgasm and death, then this theme is confirmed by the ending of the film. Here, Karlstein commits suicide in remorse at her excessive sexual drives resulting in the accidental death of her lover, played by Franco regular Jack Taylor. Irina's demise once again conflates the sexual with destruction. As she bathes in a pool of blood, her body writhes in the uncontrollable spasm of the death throes. This indicates that both death and the sex act involve a "kind of epileptic fit or temporary seizure'.[5]

In the later *Doriana Gray*, the connection between orgasm and death is split between two characters (once again played by Romay). While Doriana takes pleasure in seducing her victims before dispatching them with a similar oral sadism to Irina Karlstein, her twin experiences the displeasure that accompanies these death throes. In this respect: "*Doriana* (aka *Porno Story Of The Marquise de Sade*) is a film of climaxes. Romay squirms in a fever, seducing everyone with her lust-engorged body. As usual, she's a bisexual, who kills with her tongue, bringing her lovers to ecstasy and death."[6]

While Doriana's existence and youth are predicated on these erotic (and ultimately fatalistic) encounters, her twin suffers isolation, as well as a physical decline. As with *Female Vampire* the eventual fusion of sexual and death drives results in the destruction of both female agents after Doriana literally masturbates herself into annihilation in the film's closing stages.

In her influential book *Creativity And Perversion*, Janine Chasseguet-Smirgel has argued that the interest in sexual annihilation that marks Sade's work is one of many transgressive forms of "mixture' which dominated the writer's narratives. According to her analysis, works such as *120 Days Of Sodom*, *Justine* and *Philosophy In The Boudoir* are governed by a transgressive drive towards the dissolution of established forms: "All will be higgledy-piggledy, all will wallow on the flagstones, on the earth, and like animals will interchange, will mix, will commit incest adultery and sodomy."[7] As this above quotation from *120 Days Of Sodom* indicates, Sade's interest is seen not only in collapsing the boundary between orgasm and death, but also other crucial social and psychic boundaries. Chasseguet-Smirgel identifies these as including the dissolution of the barriers separating man from woman, adult from child, as well as one erotic zone from another. An example of Sade's policy is what she terms as a confusion between "gender and generations" in his works[8].

This relocation of sexuality within the familial (as well as the disorder and chaos that inevitably emerges from such encounters) pre-empts some of Freud's comments on the destructive capacities of the infant's sexual urges. It is the dissolution of such boundaries that affect not only the content but also the *structure* of the narrative, which in Sade, shifts to accommodate the bodies altered mode of sexual display.

For instance, his frequent construction of sexuality as a site of public performance and contemplation robs the act not only of intimations of privacy and emotion but translates eroticism into a group activity "in which protagonists build up extremely complex positions which are then unmade and transformed"[9]. Evidence of the processes of transgressive transformation that emerge from increased physiological activity includes Chasseguet-Smirgel's examples of the marriages arranged between children in *120 Days Of Sodom*. While this depiction collapses the division between infants and adults, both this and *Juliette* use these ceremonies to disturb established gender divisions by dressing men as brides and women as grooms.[10]

Alongside the corruption of those binary oppositions separating sexuality from death, as well as one gender from another, Chasseguet-Smirgel has also identified the theme "diabolical surgery" in Sade's work. Here, the medical figure utilizes methods of surgery to unite previously disparate body boundaries. In Sade's writings, the role of the transgressive surgeon takes two forms. He is depicted either as a medical figure whose direct intervention on the human form profoundly alters the established boundaries of subjectivity[11], or as a symbolic figure (such as the libertine) who arranges a series of violent or sexual displays which fuse disparate identities.

In this respect, Chasseguet-Smirgel argues that the sadean surgeon places himself in the role of god, who is able to create new forms by transmuting the established human body. This is indicated by one sadistic surgeon who states in *Justine*:

"...these portions of disorganised matter we throw into the crucible of nature, afford her the pleasure of creating anew, under different forms."[12] Franco's films reiterate the theme of the diabolical surgeon by detailing the activities of medical figures whose activities are conflated with the sexual and the perverse. This was a pattern initiated in the 1961 film *The Awful Dr Orlof*. Here, Howard Vernon is depicted as a perverse medical figure who abducts young women in order to perform skin grafts on the face of his disfigured daughter. Reiterating Sade's conflation of sexuality with violence and death it is interesting that all of Orlof's victims are prostitutes or "exotic" dancers that he courts at a disreputable club.

The film's basis in the activities of surgeons such as Rodin from *Justine* is indicated in the sadomasochistic paraphernalia that adorns Orlof's location. (These include a torture chamber where the disfigured women whom he has experimented on are chained to a wall and left to die). Orlof is assisted in his activities by a mutant killer aptly named "Morpho' because his face and physical identity have been irreparably altered by the Doctor's previously unsuccessful experiments.[13]

However, it is not merely *The Awful Dr Orlof*'s violent and literal reconstruction of the self which provides evidence of sadean mixture, but the way in which the film presents an uncanny fusion between characters with opposing traits. For instance, Orlof's eventual demise is premised on his sexual fascination with the film's heroine Wanda. After being stalked by the surgeon, she resolves to capture him, much against the wishes of her lover who is leading the police inquiry into his crimes.

Wanda's investigations lead her to the night club where he chooses prostitutes and erotic dancers as future victims. In order to entice Orlof into a confession she transforms her identity

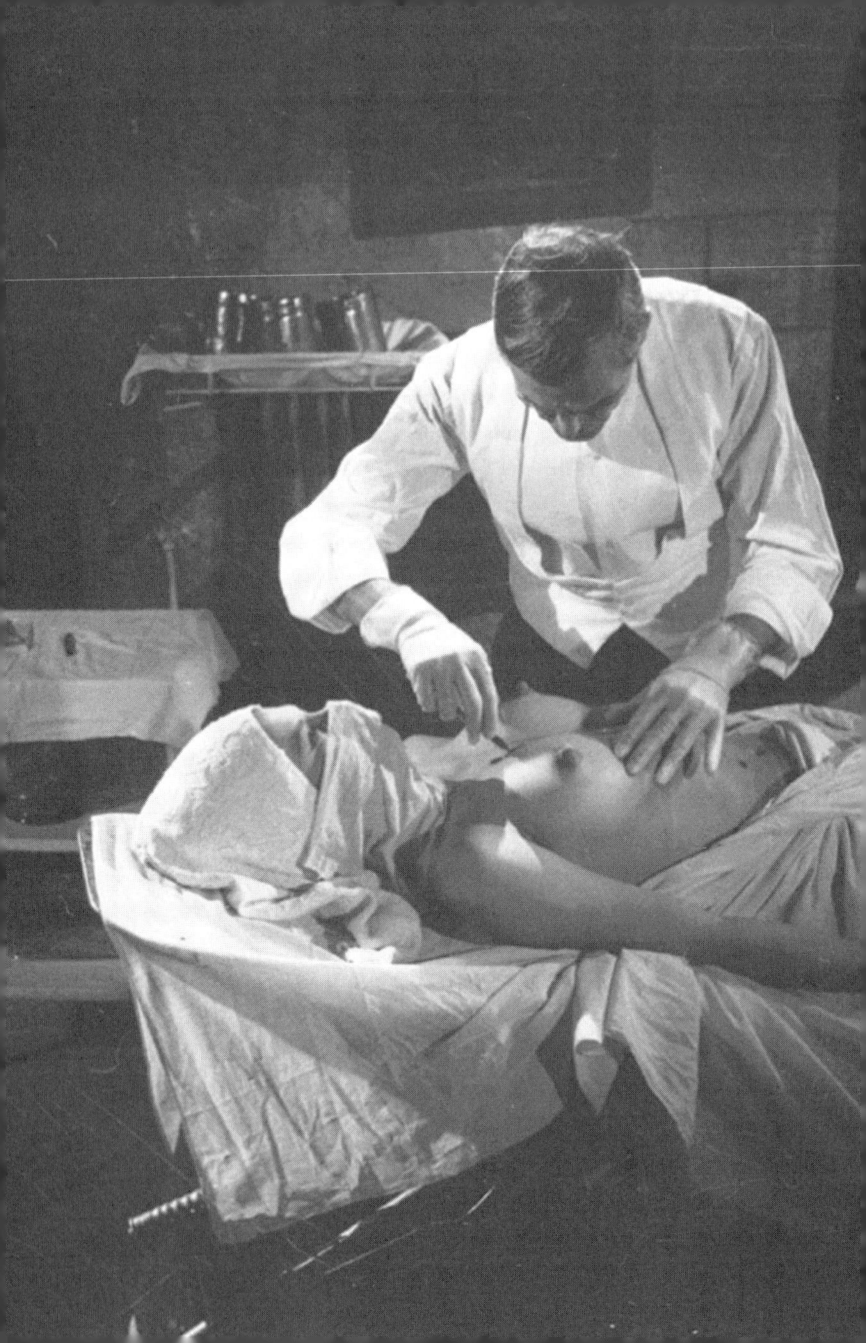

DE SADE

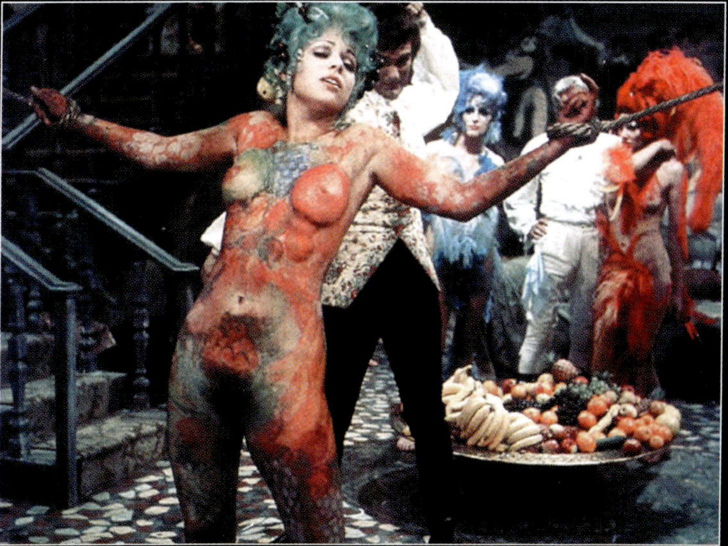

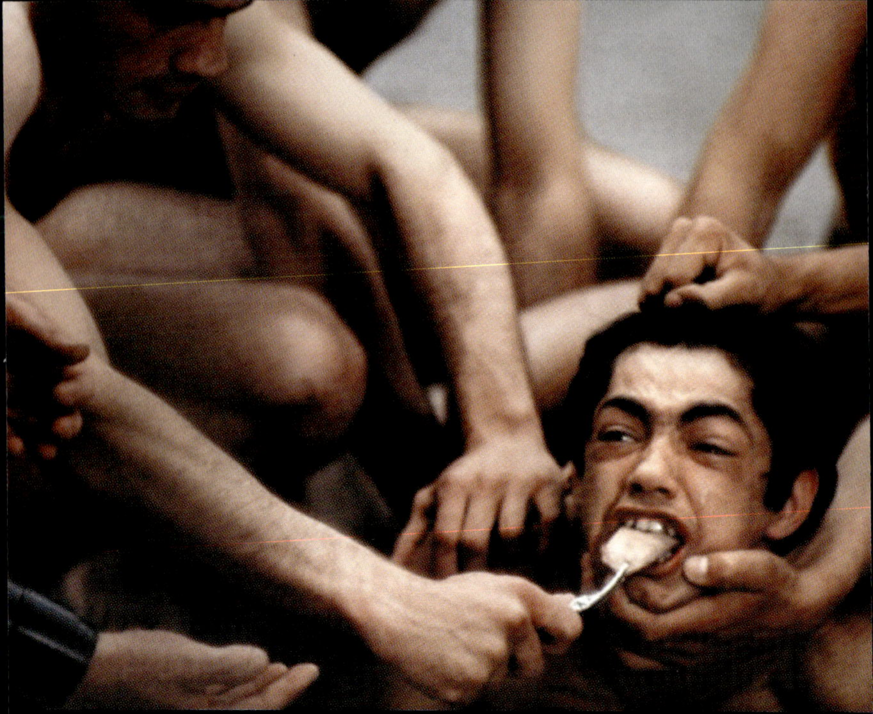

■異端文学「美徳の不幸」完璧の映画化！
マルキ・ド・サドのジュスティーヌ
〈カラー作品〉
恍惚の極致か！異常の悪徳か！
の絢爛たる〃悪の花園〃にさまよう美徳の処女ジュスティーヌ……
ジャック・パランス
ジェス・フランコ監督
マルキ・ド・サド
日本ヘラルド映画
Justine
ROMINA POWER

from a virtuous ballerina to a provocative inhabitant of the locale. Her sexual transition, in Wanda's own words, allows her to adopt the guise of a "shameless hussy', indicating the interchangeability of virtue and vice in Sade's view of sexuality. This is reflected in the interrelations between Sade's two most famous women: the sisters Justine and Juliette.

Although the two novels which detail their lives indicate shared childhood experiences, the adult lives of the two sisters are marked by disparate drives towards virtue and vice respectively. However, the fact that Juliette performs all the crimes for which Justine is accused underscores what Angela Carter argues is the reciprocity that exists between the pair. As she notes in *The Sadeian Woman*, Juliette's: "...vision of the inevitable prosperity of vice, as shown in her triumphant career, and the vision of the inevitable misfortunes of virtue that Justine's life offers... mutually reflect one another like a pair of mirrors."[14].

In its finale, *The Awful Dr Orlof* once again draws this collapsing of identity and sexuality to the theme of orgasm as death. After being captured by Morpho, Wanda discovers that the surgeon's erotic attachment to her is premised on her physical similarity to his (rapidly declining) daughter. It is this transgressive drive towards differing types of physiological "mixture' which marks not only the film (and the sequels which Franco later produced), but also his versions of other established "diabolical surgeons" as seen in *Erotic Rites Of Frankenstein* (1972) and *Jack The Ripper* (1976, starring Klaus Kinski).

Important to figures such as Orlof is not only a medical flair but the will to reproduce God's powers over physiology. They are also seen to possess an ability to verbalise the paradoxes that govern the human condition.[15] It is this duel concern with the medical and creative (thus collapsing another set of dichotomies) that defines the true status of the libertine and the surgeon in both Sade and Franco's work.

Even when depicting figures who are not strictly doctors, Franco's libertines retain an ability to transcend established body barriers through an ability to organise regimes of torture and sexual punishment. For instance, in *Ilsa The Wicked Warden* (aka *Greta The Mad Butcher*, 1977) Dianne Thorne reprises her former role of a sadistic camp warden who both mutilates and seduces her female inmates before being ripped to pieces by her former prisoners. As Tohill and Tombs have noted, her links to other Franco libertines is confirmed by not only the direction of her power towards physical violation, but also the construction of her locale around pseudo-scientific principles: "Ilsa's jail had an assortment of rooms set aside for her sadistic pleasure, some had strung-up, whipped women, others were filled with the human flotsam, the disfigured remnants of her indecent experiments."[16] The fact that libertines such as Ilsa use power to devise strategies of torture which end in bouts of copulation further confirms the theatrical basis of sexuality in Sade's writings. (While her disposal of these partners following a climax reiterates the close connection between eroticism and death).[17] If one of the logical conclusions of Sade's view of sexuality as a site of both power and spectacle is the depiction of the orgy as "the most natural form of sexual experience"[18], then it is a feature shared by many of Franco's films.

These works directly depict the orchestration of scenes of mass copulation, as in the organised orgies controlled by libertines such Ilsa or Count Dicken in *The Sadist Of Notre Dame* (1974). Equally, his works often feature locations which exploit eroticism as the site of a public spectacle, as in *Orlof* and the "Flamingo Club" of *Sadisterotica* (1968). Another related strategy which

Franco uses to render sexuality as a site of public contemplation is to use party scenes as a site where communal desires converge on the body of the text's heroine as in *Succubus* (1967) and *Venus In Furs* (1968).

Paradoxically, this public foregrounding of sexuality in Sade produces neither the emotional intensity nor the sexual pleasure associated with the erotic act. This is because for both Sade and later European thinkers such as Freud, sexual excess can never be linked to physical satisfaction or spiritual liberation. Rather, as Maurice Charney has argued, these encounters merely condemn the protagonist to endlessly repeat the conditions of humiliation and punishment that dictate the orgiastic scenario. As he states in the book *Sexual Fictions*: "Sade's gargantuan sexual imagination is not intended to provoke or inflame desire, rather the vast repetition has a numbing effect. We feel disgust and outrage much more vividly than desire."[19] Where the effect of these orgiastic and destructive encounters are most marked is in the processes of narrative repetition which dominates both Sade and Franco's work.[20] This is seen in films such as *Lady Porno* (1975) through an obsessive desire to retrace past sexual or violent events. The narrative features Lina Romay as the night club performer Sylvia, whose involvement in a love triangle results in her abduction and forced participation in both orgies and torture. Her involvement in a sadomasochistic relationship with this mysterious couple result in her being subjected to a regime of torture and sexual humilation by a wooden-legged libertine (played naturally by Franco). Upon waking, Sylvia finds that both her former lovers are dead and is she forced to flee the mansion where the activities are set.

This plot device (revealed as a contrivance in order to blackmail Sylvia into revealing details of her relations with a diplomat) establishes a process of repetition which comes to dominate the rest of the narrative. If Romay's kidnapping and torture features as an absurd trope repeated in the narrative, *Lady Porno* also confirms Timo Airaksinen's belief that sexuality in the sadean text also results in an alteration in the narrative's generic mode[21]. While Sylvia's first encounter at the mansion emphasises the degree of punishment that she endures, subsequent abductions to this locale are played much more for comic effect. Examples of this alteration of the generic system through repetition include scenes where a couple's later attempts to ravage Romay are undercut by her repeated giggling at their fumbling. A further example is seen in the "humorous instance" of her overcoming a female seducer/molester with an unmotivated karate chop.

The shift in the narrative from pornographic titillation, to murder mystery and ultimate comic absurdity, accomplishes another form of sadean "mixture", uniting previously disparate forms. It also functions to openly acknowledge the desires of its audience. This feature is indicated by the inclusion of four distinct sequences where Sylvia addresses the camera and thus the film's audience directly. As with other Franco films such as *The Awful Dr Orlof*, the first example of this takes place in the theatre where Sylvia works. Here, the sexuality of the bodies depicted are displayed in a self-conscious reference to the presence of both fictional and non-diegetic audiences. This self-reflexive strategy remains linked to Sylvia's sexual desires for the rest of the narrative. In three further inserts she addresses the audience and asks them to assess the events depicted while masturbating herself.[22]

While narratives such as *Lady Porno* demonstrate an understanding of the processes of repetition that emerge from an excess of sexuality and suffering, *Venus In Furs* (aka *Black Angel* aka *Paroxysmus)* provides a much more complex example of how the issue of orgasm as death affects the structure of Franco's works. The narrative details the impact of a past sexually violent scenario on the alienated musician[23] Jimmy (James Darren), who attempts to uncover his connection to the body of a dead woman found washed up on a beach. The corpse is revealed to be that of a woman known as Wanda Reid, whom Jimmy recalls as having been killed at a sadomasochistic party at which he was present. Jimmy's subsequent flashback reveals Wanda's oppressors to be three former friends, headed by the sadistic Prince Ahmed (Klaus Kinski). Again on sadean lines, Ahmed construct Wanda's sexual humiliation and suffering as the site of a public spectacle. However, Jimmy's implication in the violent transgression that haunts his past is indicated by his voyeuristic obsession with seeing Wanda's body stripped and then mutilated by the guests. Equally, as his voice over to the scene states, he only left the party at this point because of a fear that he was "as sick as they were".

The discovery of Wanda's body sets up a pattern of repetition around the depiction of orgasm and death which dominates the remainder of the narrative. This functions by shifting Jimmy across a range of different locations such as Istanbul and Rio, where he encounters a number of doubles of Wanda whom become his lover. Although confused by the fact that he is now the partner of a woman whom he thought had perished, the narrative reveals that Wanda is a spectre who is terrorising those connected with her demise (including Jimmy).

Through this plot device, Franco uses the figure of Wanda to create a series of connections between sexuality and death.[24]. For instance, she exacts revenge on her former oppressors by appearing to them individually as a phantasmagoric figure who

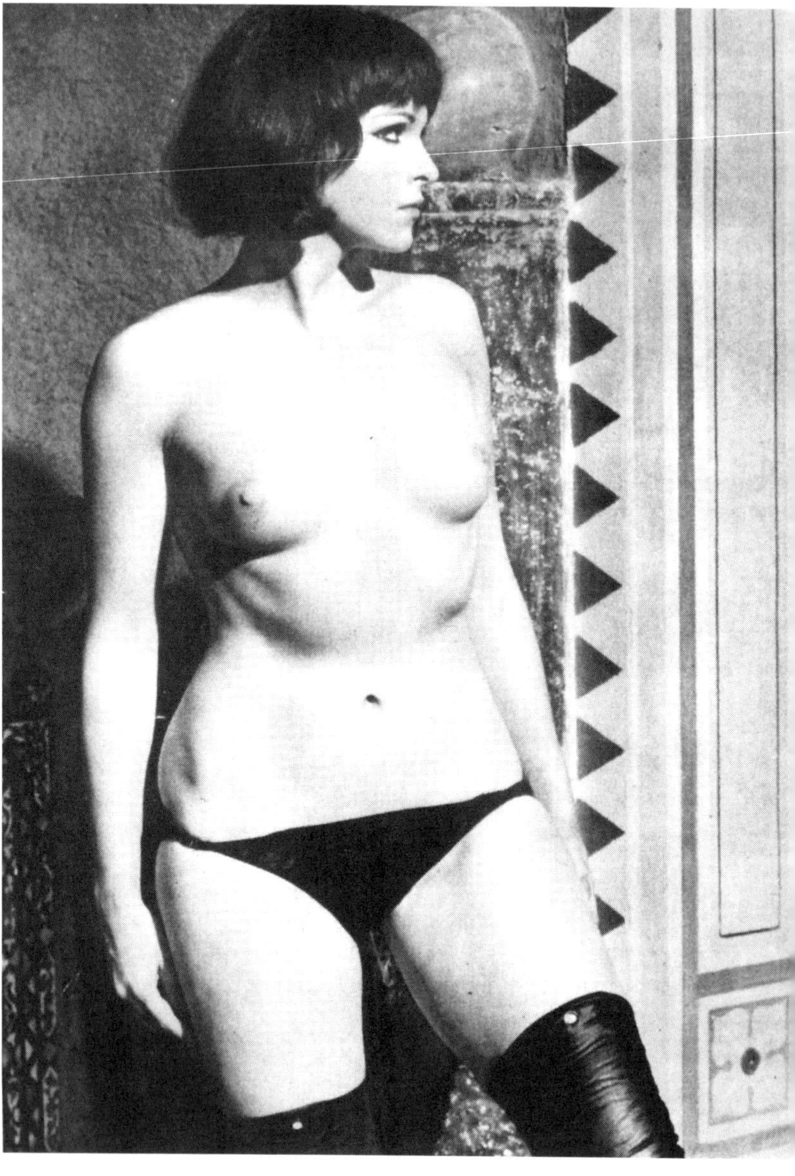

gestures further seduction only to lead them to their deaths. (Again, her appearance functions as a form of repetition which announces their demise).

An example of this is indicated in her destruction of the lesbian photographer Olga, one of the participants in her original suffering. When Olga encounters Wanda at a party and is seduced by her in front of the guests (reiterating the public as a sphere of sexuality in Franco) she presumes that she was only wounded as a result of her beating at Ahmed's party. This seduction is continued later at Olga's apartment, when Wanda appears, undresses and begins to initiate intercourse with her. It is only at the point of her climax that Olga looks down to discover that her lover is in fact the dead body that she helped mutilate at Ahmed's former gathering.

The links between narrative repetition, orgasm and annihilation are further underscored by Wanda's final encounter with Ahmed. This is a liaison which he admits is premised on his knowledge of her "from the past", as well as their being "united through death". Here Ahmed (dressed in the ceremonial robes of his ancestors) narrates another past event of how an ancient libertine attempted to win the favours of a female slave by collapsing the power distinctions which separated them. This form of social "mixture" took the reversal of their positions of authority for a limited period, culminating in their engagement in an orgiastic encounter. Importantly, when placed in a position of dominance, the former female slave (depicted once again as Wanda) introduces an element of displeasure into the coupling by forcing the bound Ahmed to watch while she seduces a series of lovers before him. Once again, the finale of this erotic encounter conflates sexuality and death as Wanda fellates her former oppressor to both the point of climax and death. According to Janine Chasseguet-Smirgel, a comprehension of Sade's work allows us a greater understanding of the sexual and destructive urges that Freud argued governed our psychic development. Importantly, the privileging of orgasm as death allows more focus to be placed on the pre-Oedipal drives which negate male control to the wishes of the mother.[25] If these early attractions emerge in later life via a connection between trauma and eroticism, their narrative effect (via a pattern of repetition) is seen in the final shots of *Venus In Furs.*

Here Jimmy, having discovered the actuality of Wanda's death, returns to his retreat in Istanbul. In a recapitulation of the film's opening shot, Franco has him discover a body washed up on the beach. In a marked contrast to the beginning of the narrative, the corpse is revealed to be that of Jimmy himself rather than Wanda. What this finale indicates is that the repetition of this past sexual and violent event do not bring liberation (as Jimmy misguidedly tells a girlfriend). Rather, they condemn the individual to sacrifice sexual pleasure for chaos and destruction. In so doing they confirm the annihilation of the barrier separating eroticism and death as a sadean feature that underpins both the content and structure of Franco's films.

2. Sade Castrated

"What an indefatigable scoundrel he is! In his first book [*Justine*] *he shows us a poor girl at bay, lost, ruined, shrinking under a rain of blows, led by inhuman monsters through one underground vault after another; from graveyard to graveyard, beaten, broken, devoured alive, wilting, crushed...When the author has committed every crime there is, when he is sated with incest and monstrosities, when he stands panting above the corpses he has stabbed and violated, when there is no church he has not sullied, no child he has not sacrificed to his rage, no moral thought on which he has not flung the foulness of his own thoughts and words, then at last this man pauses, looks at himself, smiles to himself and is not frightened."*[26]

According to Neil Schaeffer's biography *The Marquis de Sade A Life*, Donatien-Alphonse-Francois de Sade denied the authorship of *Justine*, a book he wrote in part as a response to Samuel Richardson's novel *Pamela* or *Virtue Rewarded. Justine, ou les Malheurs de la Vertu*, translated variously as the *Justine, or Misfortune of Virtue* or *Justine, or Good Conduct Well Chastised* was first published in 1791, and describes the soiled fleshy punishments endured in the life of Justine who along with her sister Juliette is abandoned to the world when her father becomes bankrupt. Forced from one humiliating, sexually violent scenario to another the twelve-year-old Justine is cut, battered, raped, buggered, tortured and abused, but always retains her virtue. Each of her brutal tormentors articulates Sadian philosophy, celebrating the pleasure of natural instincts allowed to reign free unfettered by morality, they are libertarian individualists pursuing their primal urges in a cold blackened world. In contrast

Justine throughout the cruel indignities and abuses meted out upon her body – whippings across her breasts, the endless parade of cocks into her youthful asshole, and so on – never debases her morality and never gives in to her abuser's philosophical persuasions, arguing instead that "whatever be the thorns of virtue…I prefer them unhesitatingly and always to the perilous favors which are crime's accompaniment"[27].

In marked contrast to Justine's cruel life her older sister, Juliette, when abandoned chose to become a prostitute and pursue a life of criminality and carnal satisfaction, and is wealthy and happy. At the book's climax the two sister's are reunited, and Juliette installs Justine in a country estate. At last, it appears, Justine's virtuous behaviour will be rewarded. Instead, as Justine settles into her new home, secure and happy at last, the skies darken, the wind picks-up, and a bolt of lightning smashes through the window "a blazing thunderbolt reaches her where she stands in the middle of the room…transfixes her. …the lightening entered her right breast, found the heart, and after having consumed her chest and face, burst out through her belly."[28] For Justine there is no pleasure, no satisfaction, her virtue has led to nothing but a painful, disfiguring death, struck down from above, either by a capricious supreme being or a nihilistic universe.

The most accessible of de Sade's works, *Justine* articulates his philosophy and presents various acts of sadistic sexuality in a comparatively straightforward style. It would appear to make for a relatively simple transition from literature to film. And yet, despite this Jess Franco's 1968 film *Justine* (aka *Marquis de Sade's Justine*), although gleefully enjoyable as an exercise in trash entertainment, does not succeed as an adaptation of de Sade.

The film opens with a lengthy scene of de Sade (played by

an impassive Klaus Kinski)[29] being imprisoned. Against an overblown dramatic score de Sade picks up his quill and begins to write the story of Justine. From hereon the story largely follows the sequence of events presented in de Sade's novel.

Justine and her sister Juliette are evicted from their convent school, their father unable to pay the schools fees. Both are given one-hundred crowns. Juliette takes her sister to a brothel, but Justine, horrified by the prospect of prostitution, and anxious to retain her precious virginity, leaves to wonder the streets of Paris. A monk soon takes her money and cons her into becoming a maid for a hideous landlord Du Harpin. That night, as she removes her dress and starts to weep at her misfortune the film cuts to show Juliette indulging in lesbian sex.

The comparison of the lives of the two sisters continues throughout the film, with Justine's innocent misery contrasted with Juliette's 'evil' successes. While moral Justine suffers, amoral Juliette murders and robs her way to success.

The film cuts back to de Sade in his cell, "Must it always be that disaster dogs the heels of virtue?" he asks in voice over. On the extra-diagetic soundtrack there is a fanfare of trumpets. Breaking down the distinction between verisimilitude and the pleasures of cinema, the sound appears to startle de Sade although in the narrative he is unable to hear it. As the camera tracks around the cell de Sade moves across the room, towards a phantasmagoric apparition of two naked women, nude female dreams that drive the infamous prisoner to weeping. These overacted scenes of de Sade's incarceration punctuate the film, serving to remind us that de Sade is the author of the text, and distancing the viewer from identifying with any character or the narrative trajectory.

Falsely accused of theft by Desroches, Justine is

imprisoned. Here she parties with the other women, dancing and laughing, while guards watch from high on the prison's walls. She escapes with a fellow convict, Madame Dusbois – who likes Justine because she "looks so innocent" – and flees Paris for the nearby woods. Here Dusbois offers Justine the chance of joining her gang, but rather than renounce their libertarian philosophy in favour of virtue as she does in the book, Justine maintains her innocence via silence. This tactic is repeated throughout the film, so that Justine is described as innocent or virtuous, but never fully articulates her position. The men of the gang decide to rape her, but come to blows over who should deflower her, in the confusion Justine escapes.

Fleeing the gang Justine meets and falls in love with an artist Raymond. She willingly posses naked for his paintings, although the relationship is never consummated. However she is forced to flee by a party of soldiers searching for her.

Running away she comes across two men: Jasmin and de Bressac, who employs her as a lady in waiting to his wife the Marquise. However de Bressac wants Justine to murder his wife, instead Justine confesses all to her, who tests the poison on her pet dog which lays down, and presumably dies. They are unaware that her suspicious husband is watching. He double-crosses his wife and she is poisoned. As she slowly dies he ravishes her, declaring his excitement for making love to somebody who is dying. Unfortunately she dies after only a kiss, thus negating any necrophilic rape or any true celebration of his libertine excess. De Bressac brands Justine on the breast – actually between her breasts – with an M so that, despite her innocence, she is permanently marked as the murderer of his wife.

Justine next finds herself seeking sanctuary with four evil monks. Along with other women these monks abuse and

torture Justine, in a sequence that includes acupuncture – driving thin metal needles into her quivering flesh, as well as European sex and horror staples vampiric lesbianism and bondage. Multiple images and double exposures add a psychedelic aspect to her submission at the hands of the feral clergymen. Amongst the shots of blood trickling down Justine's arms, and smeared over her trembling legs, the multiple exposures emphasise de Sade's furiously writing quill, positioning it against images of Justine's writhing body as she is chained to a dungeon wall. Close ups of her face, flesh and chains emphasise a sense of orgiastic dislocation. These are cut with images of the head monk Antonin (a brilliantly off-kilter Jack Palance) talking gibberish and slurring quasi-Sadian dialogue about searching for "what we do not know".

In one of the few moments of pseudo-philosophy in the film Antonin accuses Justine of obtaining pleasure through passively enduring her suffering, effectively reversing the dialectic, so that Justine is a sinner and he is a man of virtue. He plans to slay Justine. As thunder rolls, the monks hold a black mass in order to sacrifice Justine, but, suddenly the roof of their church caves in, its collapse offering her the chance to escape. The cinematic emphasis on the supernatural / elemental implies that divine intervention has saved Justine. This is further emphasised when, given the twilight hour and echoes of thunder heard immediately before the church's collapse, Justine flees into bright sunlight.

Finally Justine meets Raymond who once again saves her. But Dubois arrives and kidnaps Justine, while mocking her religion. Justine is forced to undergo a further indignity, working as a nude model in a freak show cum theatre. Paraded naked on stage, the crowd see the mark of the brand and heckle, driving her off stage. The mob bellowing their horror at the M on her chest she is arrested, but as she is being taken away Juliette arrives. Now wealthy, she demands to speak to her abused sister. Juliette tells that she has indulged in decadence and is wealthy having engaged in wickedness. Promising Justine happiness the two sisters leave for the countryside.

In church Justine prays. The character de Sade's authorial voice over states: "for indeed true happiness can only be found in the practice of virtue. And if God permits the righteous to be persecuted on Earth it is only to prepare them for a great reward... in Heaven." Justine leaves the church.

In his cell de Sade slumps forward, his writing completed.

The film's tone is primarily camp, from the stammering Du Harpin to the slurred Antonin, the manic leader of the evil monks, such characters are absurd exaggerations. While there is a level of humour in de Sade it cannot simply be reduced to exaggerated camp, yet the film transforms Justine's first physical punishment, a spanking, into a sequence that unwittingly recalls the English sex comedies of the sixties and seventies. The spanking is played for laughs rather than as an example of violent abuse enacted upon her struggling body for the grim sexual satisfaction of her tormentor. Simultaneously her near-rape at the hands of Dubois's gang is staged as a Three Stooges style slapstick fight between the horny men, and is largely devoid of any sense of threat or the imminent sexual horror of gang rape. This 'sense of fun' is further added to by the non-diagetic soundtrack with its fake-baroque score. The later, more brutal punishments enacted upon her flesh are more seriously presented, but the actress's performance is so poor that finally the viewer remains largely indifferent.

The stylistic excess is further emphasized with the use of intense red and green lighting, which is repeated at various times as the heroine is thrust into the (groping) hands of lustful libertines. The exaggerated performances and highly constructed

mise-en-scene create an atmosphere during Justine's interactions with her tormentors that owes more to the spectacle of gaudy horror movies than to the literary source. This bastard mixture of gothic-camp may work well for European trash cinema, but in the context of *Justine* it merely strips the narrative of de Sade's stylistic power.

While de Sade could be superficially read as camp in the excesses of the degradations he devises, to read him as such fails to appreciate his radical philosophical perspective and serves merely to reduce his litany of sadistic excess to mere affect rather than the locus for unrestricted libido. In Franco's *Justine* Sadian sexuality is reduced to a shadow of its true excess. This becomes even more absurd as the sex encounters presented in the film are so safe, reduced to mere flashes of nudity and breasts, even the film's brief foray into sadism at the hands of the monks becomes effectively safe via the use of optical effects.

In de Sade's *Justine* the heroine is rescued by her sister but is then struck with lightning, but in Franco's version it is God that rescues Justine from the murderous clutches of the crazed libertine monks. Later her faith is rewarded. Under Franco's direction de Sade is rendered to merely a name, a signifier of supposedly perverse sexuality for marketing purposes, there is little of the radical nature of de Sade in the film, his work remains only in the broad narrative and the film's title.

The Marquis de Sade's masterwork – *120 Days of Sodom* – becomes a list of sexual deviations, challenging the reader not just in content but by the very breakdown of the form of the novel itself. In his other works *Justine*, *Juliette*, and *Philosophy in the Boudoir*, the structure may be more immediately recognizable, but the furious sexuality and libertarian philosophy that defines *120 Days* is still apparent. De Sade's strength is that he writes for himself, there is no sense of seeking approval, of satisfying the audience. To read de Sade is to become implicated in his fantasies, it is to wallow, to see humanity at its most 'disturbed'. Yet this complicity is eradicated in the film. In framing the film with images of an incarcerated de Sade the film allows the audience to maintain a critical distance from the actions depicted. This sense of framing is repeated in the film at key points, allowing the audience to keep a distance, reminded that what is happening on screen is merely a story within a story.

The most realised screen version of de Sade's work is Pasolini's *Salo* [see next chapter], a film that effectively presents de Sade in a manner that still has the raw power to stun, arouse, and repel audiences. Franco by contrast has turned de Sade into an exploitation joke, in a film that may be an amusing example of Euro trash sexploitation but fails as an interpretation of de Sade's "delicious force"[30].

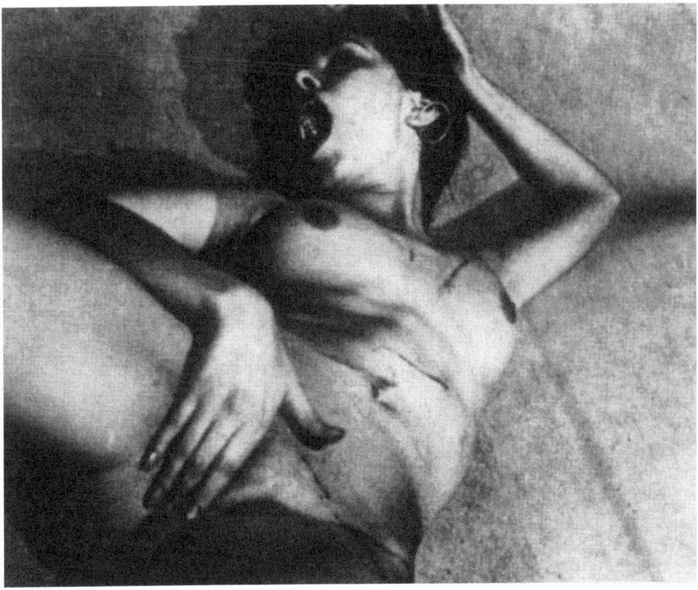

Postscript

In contrast to Franco's period version of *Justine*, his later *De Sade's Juliette* (1975) is a modern-day psycho-sexual drama with scant relation to the book – at least in its final version, which was substantially recut by Joe d'Amato[31], features hardcore scenes with Lina Romay, and is also known variously as *Justine*, *Justine And The Whip* and *Julietta 69*. A strange fugue of empty sexual encounters leading to suicide, there is little sadean about the film save for a series of brief whipping scenes. D'Amato edited in sequences from other Franco films, such as *The Shining Sex* (1976), and the result is fairly incomprehensible, functioning more as a thanato-erotic dream – although Romay, with a shaven pubis and shiny boots, looks stunning throughout.

Notes

1. Outlined in his important paper "Beyond The Pleasure Principle" (in Freud's *On Metapsychology*, Harmondsworth: Penguin, 1984).

2. For a fuller account of this case study see "From The History Of An Infantile Neurosis" in Freud's *Case Histories II*; Harmondsworth: Penguin, 1981.

3. Sade's influences, both directly and through movements such as surrealism on Franco are most clearly examined in Kevin Collins' exhaustive interview with the director contained in Craig Ledbetter's *European Trash Cinema* (Special Edition #1), October 1996.

4. One important example of this is the sado-masochistic stage routine performed by the sexually confused heroine Lorna (Janine Reynaud) in *Succubus* (1967).

5. Maurice Charney, p38.

6. Cathal Tohill and Pete Tombs, *Immoral Tales: Sex And Horror Cinema In Europe 1956-1984*; London: Primitive Press, 1994, p119.

7. Sade, *120 Days Of Sodom*, p56 (cited in Janine Chasseguet-Smirgel, *Creativity And Perversion*; London: Free Association Books, 1992.

8. Chasseguet-Smirgel's conclusion that sexuality is used as a tool to subvert established power structures in Sade is pertinent. She notes that this inversion is seen in his *Philosophy In The Boudoir*, which with its subtitle "Teachers Of Immorality – Dialogues For The Education Of Young Ladies" subverts the notion of the educator as guardian of the moral welfare of the children in their charge. Indeed, it is not merely that youth is introduced to vice via contact with these older instructors, but as *120 Days Of Sodom* indicates, they also suffer punishment and violation as part of this initiation. Franco's cinema often follows this Sadeian root by depicting female characters who suffer sadism at the hands of mentors. Examples of this type of narrative include *Love Letters Of A Portuguese Nun* (1978), which features William Berger as a head priest who castigates young women for their inability to resist temptations of the flesh only then to molest them when they are sent to his convent for repentance.

9. Ibid., p2–3.

10. This last example is a point more fully explored by Angela Carter in *The Sadeian Woman*; (London: Virago, 1990).

11. Chasseguet-Smirgel gives the example of the sadistic surgeon Rodin from Justine who places himself in the position of God by creating new physical forms through direct medical intervention. As she notes, the operation he performs on his daughter involves the removal of her womb, effectively deleting fertility as a key feature which separates masculine from feminine.

12. Ibid., p4.

13. This inclusion of the mutant as Orlof's assistant itself provides a point of textual mixture of fusion between the two. Although Orlof's character is depicted as a rational counterfoil to Morpho's brutality the two are continually conflated by both the police and public assisting in the enquiry. An example of this is seen in the scene where an artist's impression of both men causes consternation in the crowd, who believe they have seen the same man attempting to abduct women in the city.

14. Angela Carter, p79.

15. The connection is confirmed by Orlof's assumption of the role of a libertine (whose function Sade saw as to contemplate the nature of love, morality and ethics) when depicted in the bar. In one scene he uses his attempts to seduce a prostitute with references to her good looks to launch into a monologue on the inevitable link between beauty and decay.

16. Cathal Tohill & Pete Tombs, *Immoral Tales: Sex And Horror Cinema In Europe 1956-1984*, p115.

17. Equally, the film's most controversial scene, which involves the forced consumption of faeces by a prisoner, reiterates Chasseguet-Smirgel's emphasis on pre-Oedipal states such as anality in Sade.

18. Charney, p33.

19. Ibid., p53.

20. An example of this process of repetition through copulation is given in *Juliette*. Here, a narrative sub-plot surrounding the heroine's capture by various male aggressors (such as a cannibal and a brigand chief) is repeated to ensure Juliette's freedom through her participation in further orgies. Importantly, during these encounters, Juliette is aided by female characters such as Clairwell, confirming Angela Carter's view that Sade's heroines are constructed through a subversion of male power.

21. In his book *The Philosophy Of The Marquis De Sade*; London: Routledge, 1995. The importance of Airaksinen's work is the emphasis he places on the narrative alteration that Sade's orgasm as death trait provokes.

22. The preoccupation of Franco's heroines towards acts of auto-eroticism once again confirms the contradiction around identity and sexuality in Sade's writings. Although characters such as Sylvia function as the classic Sadeian "whore', their pleasure extends far beyond the mere servicing of the male characters that these works depict. Rather, they show an ambivalence towards male sexual power recalling some of the dominant women that populate narratives such as *Juliette*. For instance, Angela Carter has noted the heroine's gravitation towards characters such as the nymphomaniac Madame de Clairwell, whose sexual pleasure is premised on masturbation and the use of vibrators. In so doing, Carter argues that this character combines an excess of sexual desire with a rejection of the male in preference for the "disembodied' phallus. Arguably, Sylvia's mocking attitude towards her two male lovers is indicated in her continued evasion of their attempted seductions. Irina Karlstein of *The Female Vampire* also maintains an ambivalent relationship to male potency. Although the phallus is her favoured object of achieving the orgasm as death trope that Franco's films detail, her own sexual pleasure is premised on masturbation, which the film reveals as separate to her interactions with male lovers.

23. The fact that the narrative depicts Jimmy as a jazz musician is important. Not only does it reflect Franco's much noted interest in this musical genre, but it also indicates this type of composition to be a form which is open to the "mixing" of different styles. It is interesting to note that Chasseguet-Smirgel refers to certain types of free form music as being "open to deviation from established tonal structures.

24. As Franco discusses in his interview with Kevin Collins in *European Trash Cinema*, certain named characters reoccur across his texts. Beyond the

obvious example of Dr Orlof, characters such as Morpho have also appeared as barbaric henchmen in films such as *Sadisterotica*. From a Sadeian perspective this degree of overlap indicates that repetition is occurring both within and between Franco films.

25. According to Maurice Charney, the importance of the mother's body to the child's sexual drives are evidenced by a speech given by Clément, one of the libertines from *Justine*: "It is in the mother's womb that there are fashioned the organs which must render us susceptible of such-and-such a fantasy; the first objects which we encounter, the first conversations we overhear determine the pattern; once tastes are formed nothing in the world can destroy them." (Cited in *Sexual Fictions*, p51.)

26. Jules Janin, 'Revue de Paris', 1834, cited in Georges Bataille, *Eroticism*, Marion Boyars: London, 1987 (1962), p.177.

27. Marquis de Sade, *Justine, Philosophy in the Bedroom, and Other Writings*, Arrow Books Limited: London, 1991, p.481.

28. Marquis de Sade, *Justine, Philosophy in the Bedroom, and Other Writings*, Arrow Books Limited: London, 1991, p.741-742..

29. Kinski was once again due to play the Marquis in a 1975 production, *Sade*, to be directed by Jean Chérasse, but the project never came to fruition. The script was based on Chérasse's published text *Sade, J'Ecris Ton Nom: Liberté*, co-written with Geneviéve Guicheney.

30. Marquis de Sade, *The Ghosts of Sodom: The Charenton Journals*, Creation Books: London, 2003, p.111.

31. The primary Franco footage was shot for an aborted remake of **Justine**, in 1975. An original **Juliette**, starring Soledad Miranda in the title role, was started by Franco in 1970 but never completed; not only was the money running out, but only around 40 minutes of material had been shot when Miranda was killed in a car-crash on the highway to Lisbon.

III

PASOLINI AND SADE: A MALEFICENT OBSESSION

1. Ante-Inferno

Salò is the unique space where film terminally collides with death.

'Death does determine life, I feel that, and I've written it, too, in one of my recent essays, where I compare death to film-montage. Once life is finished, it acquires a sense; up to that point it has not got a sense; its sense is suspended and therefore ambiguous...For me, death is the maximum of epicness and myth.'[1]

–Pier Paulo Pasolini, 1968

2.
Circle of Obsessions

During the production in 1975 of what would be his ultimate film, *Salò* – adapted from Sade's novel *120 Days of Sodom* and transposed to the final moments of the fascist dictatorship in mid-1940s Italy – the film-maker and poet Pier Paulo Pasolini often asserted that he wanted that film to be 'the last movie'[2]: not only his own last movie, but also that of the entire human species: a film of terminal images, before the processes of cultural and social erasure which Pasolini incessantly denounced had engulfed and nullified the visual image entirely. The images of *Salò* – revelatory of the structures of cruelty and of the sexual origins of human atrocities and massacres – would then form a kind of malign legacy, left for any non-human species which, at some point in the future, might want to look back upon the memories and obsessions of the human species. The concept of the 'last film' was one that attracted many other film-makers during the era of tumultuous upheaval, revolutionary terrorism and worldwide violence that extended from the mid-1960s to the late-1970s; in the USA, the actor-director Dennis Hopper had already adopted that notion of a 'last movie' for the film-title of his seminal, drug-disintegrated masterwork of 1971. However, *Salò* was not the first Pasolini film to be conceived of as a terminal exercise; like his contemporary, the West German director Rainer Werner Fassbinder, Pasolini was perpetually announcing his abandonment of film-making, while simultaneously planning another film-project that would push beyond the extreme limit of his current film. Similarly, the novelist Jean Genet – a profound source of inspiration for Pasolini – declared in *The Thief's Journal* (1949) that it would be his last novel, then asserted in that novel's final two sentences that it would, after all, have a sequel (which never actually transpired). For Pasolini, that film beyond-the-end was to have been a project entitled *Porno-Teo-Kolossal*, which was in preparation to be shot, in New York, Naples and Paris, in the first months of 1976, based on a 75-page film-treatment largely composed of dialogue. However, whether by chance or intention, *Salò* would mark the very end of Pasolini's work – shortly after he had finished editing it, he was savagely murdered by a boy-hustler whose penis he had been sucking only minutes earlier.

Salò was a terminal aberration in Pasolini's work. Unusually, he took on a project which he had not developed himself; his collaborator Sergio Citti had initiated the project, intending to direct it himself, but could not find a producer for it. Pasolini had no difficulty in attracting the producer Alberto Grimaldi, who had had an immense success with *Last Tango in Paris*, directed three years earlier by Bernardo Bertolucci. Once Pasolini had taken on the project, at the beginning of 1975, he researched it intensively; alongside Sade's own work, he read essays on Sade by Georges Bataille (notably, Bataille's preface to Sade's book), Roland Barthes, Pierre Klossowski and Maurice Blanchot, as well as conducting research into the last phase of Italian fascism. And in August 1975, following the film's shooting-period, he would meet with the Surrealist artist Man Ray, who had painted an 'imaginary portrait' of Sade in 1938; Pasolini was contemplating using the portrait on posters for his film.

The Marquis de Sade's *120 Days of Sodom* details the acts of four atheistic Parisian 'libertines' who possess the wealth and power to realize a plan to have sixteen aristocratic young boys and girls kidnapped from their homes, and brought to an isolated castle in Switzerland, the Castle of Silling; accompanied by four story-tellers and eight well-endowed 'cockmongers', the libertines spend four months inflicting an escalating series of sexual tortures on the boys and girls, before finally slaughtering them and returning to Paris. The boys and girls to be massacred are all selected for their exceptional beauty (especially that of their rear-ends), for their young age (between twelve and fifteen), and for their social origins: Augustine, for example, is described by Sade as 'fifteen years old; daughter of a Languedoc baron, with an alert and pretty face'[3]. Sade completed his account of the first of the four months, November, while imprisoned for acts of debauchery at the Bastille prison in Paris in 1785. However, the remaining three parts of the book (for the months of December to February) were only written in the form of notational drafts: skeletal enumerations of the acts undertaken by the libertines, and cryptic summaries of the accompanying story-tellers' narratives. It appears that Sade intended to publish the first part of the book separately, and then to complete each of the three other parts as the publication progressed; however, the manuscript, written on a long scroll of paper, was lost during the revolutionary riots of 1789, and only re-discovered in the early twentieth century. The French Revolution changed Sade's fortunes: released from the Bastille, he initially became a revolutionary judge (though a lenient one, who rarely condemned anyone brought before him), but then fell into poverty and ended his life in the benign incarceration of the Charenton asylum-hospital, on the edge of Paris.

Pasolini moved the action of the novel in time, to the period 1944-45, thirty years prior to the moment of the film's making. He also moved the action geographically, from an impregnable, mountain-top castle in Switzerland to a salubrious lake-side villa in the small resort town of Salò, overlooking a bay on the Riviera Bresciana, on the banks of Lake Garda in northern Italy. It was in Salò that the Italian fascist dictator Benito

Mussolini (who had held power since the year of Pasolini's birth, 1922) established his short-lived 'Republic of Salò' with his remaining supporters. Although Mussolini does not appear as a character in Pasolini's film, his desperate, extreme situation of that period is omnipresent; his 'Republic of Salò' was a final pocket of fascism, ready to defend itself at all costs, by acts of atrocity, after the Italian government had concluded a surrender with the British and American forces, thereby changing sides in the last phase of the Second World War. The Italian government had then deposed and imprisoned Mussolini in 1943, confining him to a hotel on the inaccessible peak of the Gran Sasso mountain in the Abruzzo region, east of Rome, expecting to be able to try him at the end of the war; but Mussolini's friend and ally, Adolf Hitler, was determined to rescue Mussolini from Gran Sasso, and dispatched his best pilot to land on the mountain-peak and spirit Mussolini away to the Lake Garda region, which was still held by the German forces. Mussolini was then installed as the dictator of the northern part of Italy still under the control of the Germans, while the invading British and American forces were rapidly advancing northwards through Italy, after landing in Sicily. As that advance reached the north, Mussolini's chaotic 'Republic of Salò' quickly disintegrated; on the run from partisans, he was captured and cursorily machine-gunned to death in April 1945, in a village alongside Lake Como, then hung upside-down, alongside his mistress, in the Piazzale Loreto in Milan. News of the ignominy of Mussolini's killing led Hitler to commit suicide, in order to avoid meeting a similar fate, as Josef Stalin's Soviet army closed-in on Hitler's own headquarters in Berlin.

Pasolini knew the Salò region of Lake Garda well, and had lived for a time in that area in his youth (his father was a professional soldier: in fact, a professional fascist, and the father's military postings had meant that the Pasolini family had moved constantly from one region of northern Italy to another, during Pasolini's youth). Pasolini also had intimate personal knowledge of the atrocities committed by the Italian fascists on the civilian population during the final stages of the conflict; he had witnessed the aftermath of acts of mass execution. In an interview about his film's location in space and time, he said: 'It was an epoch of sheer cruelty, searches, executions, deserted villages, all totally useless, and I suffered a great deal.'[4] During the period in which *Salò* is set, Pasolini's only brother, Guido, was executed at the age of twenty, in March 1945, in the course of his anti-fascist guerrilla activities, first wounded and captured along with his group of partisans, then coldly finished-off with a bullet in the head; after the war was over, Pasolini learned that his brother had died uselessly – he had not been killed by the Nazis or Italian fascists after all, but instead had been executed as the result of a chaotic squabble between two rival anti-fascist partisan groups.

In writing the film-script for *Salò*, Pasolini made a number of significant changes in the characters of Sade's novel; in particular, he placed more emphasis on the four libertines' social position. In Sade's novel, the libertines are obstinate outsiders who, despite their colossal wealth, exist on the disgraced periphery of eighteenth-century French society, and are largely oblivious to it, except to the degree that it can provide them with human materials for their projects of sexual torture and slaughter. But the libertines of *Salò*, inflected by Pasolini's idiosyncratic version of Marxism, are conceived as 'types', and are clearly fully complicit both with Mussolini's fascist project, and with Italian society in general. The young girls and boys brought to the libertines' villa in *Salò* have all been captured at gunpoint, from peasant farms and wretched urban areas; they are the opposite of

Sade's rarefied cast of the abducted children of aristocrats and wealthy military officers.

Despite that difference in emphasis in the social status of the characters in *Salò* and *120 Days of Sodom*, there are close correspondences between the figures of Sade and Pasolini. Even before his imprisonment in the Bastille, Sade had been burned in effigy in the market-place of Aix-en-Provence, after fleeing to Italy to escape being executed for his crimes of sexual debauchery. At the time when *Salò* was made, the openly-homosexual Pasolini had already spent twenty years being reviled by the Italian media for his sexual and political declarations, as well as for the experimentation of his films and books; even in death, he would be assailed and ridiculed by the Italian right-wing media, which unashamedly relished his murder (just as the West German media would relish Fassbinder's cocaine-induced death, seven years later). And both Sade and Pasolini sought, in their disparate ways, to discover means to finally detonate the narratives and foundations of social power-systems.

Pasolini finished the script for *Salò* in February 1975, working with his collaborators Sergio Citti and Pupi Avati. After its casting-sessions, the film was shot very rapidly, over the course of thirty-seven days, from 3 March to 14 April 1975, in a villa near the city of Mantua, not far to the south of the town of Salò. The film was shot with a cast that mixed young, inexperienced actors with veterans of the Italian film-industry, some of them familiar character-actors who would go on to appear in the wave of late-1970s chic Nazi-porn exploitation films which Pasolini's own film unwittingly helped to spark. Before the shooting of each scene, Pasolini only gave instructions at the last moment to the young actors and actresses (most of them non-professionals, who never appeared in any subsequent films) playing the captive boys and girls, thereby inducing an authentic sense of unease and disquiet in their performances. The only break in the gruelling shoot came when Pasolini discovered that Bernardo Bertolucci (whose films, including *Last Tango in Paris*, he detested as crowd-pleasing, consumerist fodder) was shooting his current film, *1900*, in the nearby countryside around Mantua; Bertolucci had briefly served as Pasolini's assistant on a previous film, and *1900* was being produced by the same producer, Alberto Grimaldi, as *Salò*. The football-obsessed Pasolini immediately challenged Bertolucci to a game between the two casts; however, in the subsequent match, marked by violence, the *Salò* cast (captained by the fifty-three-year-old Pasolini, and including the young actors playing the well-endowed 'cockmongers') unexpectedly lost 3-6 to the *1900* team, and Pasolini left the pitch several minutes before the end of the game, exhausted and cursing. Once the filming had been completed, Pasolini moved to other commitments in his writing of fiction, poetry and journalism, returning to the project in early October 1975 to edit it (as with the cinematography of the film, its raw editing shows signs of having been accomplished urgently, while Pasolini's obsessions were still lividly alive), and then travelled to Sweden for screenings of his previous films, and to Paris to prepare a French-language version of *Salò*, before arriving back in Rome on 31 October, the day before his death.

Pasolini was aware that, in many ways, the obscenity and uncompromising cruelty of *Salò* formed a complete break from his earlier films. Although some of those films, especially his first film, *Accatone* (1961), had created scandals of their own, Pasolini knew that *Salò* constituted a new kind of film-making for him. As a result, in 1975, he publicly 'denounced' his previous three films, in order to clear the ground for the reception of *Salò*. Pasolini's previous films had often presented positive and dignified depictions of the poor; in *Salò*, by contrast, the poor and defenceless subjects of torture and slaughter would be relentlessly degraded and excoriated, their status as passive 'victims' provocatively set under interrogative questioning, in order to dismantle it.

Pasolini expected the first screenings of the film to create a furore throughout Europe, and to bring down unprecedented media attacks upon him. He noted: '*Salò* goes so far beyond the limits that those who ordinarily speak badly of me will have to find a new language.'[5] But by the time the film was screened, Pasolini was dead. *Salò* had initially been refused a visa by the Italian censorship board, then passed on 23 December 1975; it was projected in Italian cinemas during the period when newspaper photographs of Pasolini's murdered body – the corpse lying on its front, the mud-caked vest pushed up to reveal its naked back, its chest and head exploded into a pool of blood – were still being avidly consumed by the country's population. After being shown for only three weeks, *Salò* was abruptly withdrawn; for the next three decades, the film faced suppression and censorship-battles in numerous countries around the world, without the presence of Pasolini to defend its driving obsessions.

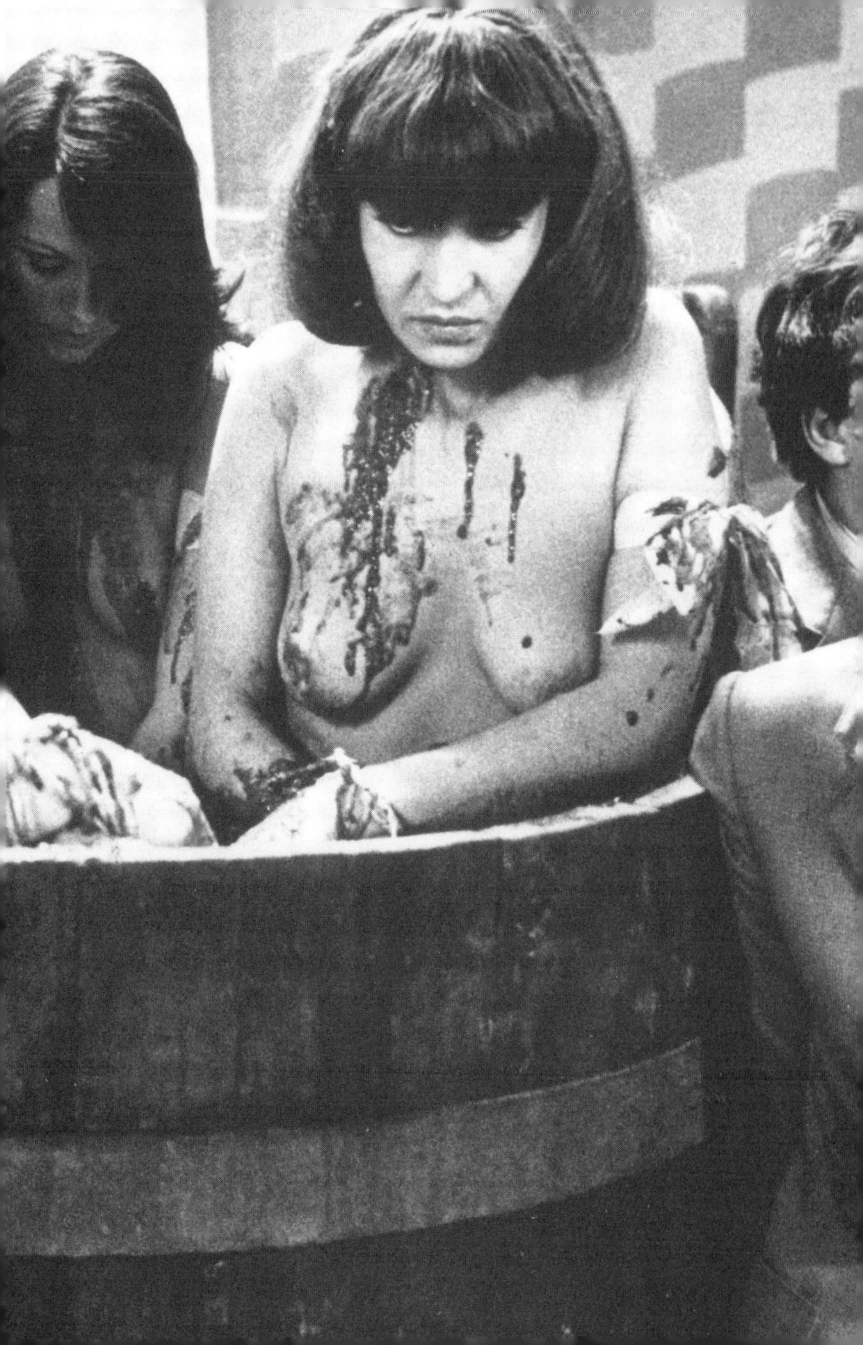

3.
Circle of Shit

The core of *Salò* is the anus, and its narrative drive pivots around the act of sodomy; no scene of a sex act has been confirmed, in the film, until one of the libertines has approached its participants and sodomized the figure committing that act. The filmic material of *Salò* is one that compacts celluloid and shit, in Pasolini's desire to burst the limits of cinema, via the anally resonant eye of the film-lens. In order to achieve an inciting relentlessness in his narrative, and to engulf his victims in the aura of excrement emanated by the film, Pasolini intersects his images with puncture-points of story-tellers' narration. Those story-tellers' sequences in *Salò* carry a more tangential role than that in *120 Days of Sodom*, where they possess a status equal with that of the libertines' acts, in Sade's double-barrelled narrative-technique. In *Salò*, the story-tellers' narratives solely carry the momentum which propels the film's passive victims and viewers into its infernal 'circle of shit'.

In *120 Days of Sodom*, Sade's libertines are all eager shit-eaters, constantly provoking the captive boys and girls to deposit ever-larger consignments of excrement into their mouths, thereby also escalating the number of sex acts which the libertines can accomplish. But the inspiration of Sade's obsession with the human anus extended much further than that of shit-eating, in his influence upon the French Surrealist movement in the 1930s, and on film-makers and theorists of the postwar era, from Pasolini to Gilles Deleuze and Jean Baudrillard. The seminal element in Sade which proved so inspirational is his profound preoccupation with violent anatomical manipulation, with its focus on the anus; once the human body has been radically re-configured, it is in a state of volatile flux which renders it more resistant or unrecuperable to stratified power-formations. In Sade, that reconfiguration of the body is simultaneously both an act of corporeally-endowed power, and the annulment or overturning of that entire structure of power; for example, a libertine, in Sade's book, severs the flesh-partition between a girl's anus and vagina, so that she is forced to defecate through her vagina.

Pasolini faltered in his desire to make the young actors and actresses of the *Salò* cast commit un-simulated sodomy and to eat actual excrement, serving them instead a palatable mix of chocolate and orange marmalade, which he retrospectively justified as a material which helped to adhere his film's ability to make connections between elements of consumerism and fascism (in which consumption, even of excrement, is never authentic, and is always the result of a fascistic simulation of the kind denounced by Baudrillard and the Situationist theorists). Until the expansion of the hard-core pornographic industry into shit-eating films at the end of the 1970s, it had been left to experimental film-makers – notably Kurt Kren and Otto Muehl, of the Vienna Action Group, with their seminal work *Scheisskerl* (1970) – to demonstrate that excrement could be eaten, and that act combined with an explicit sex-act, on film.

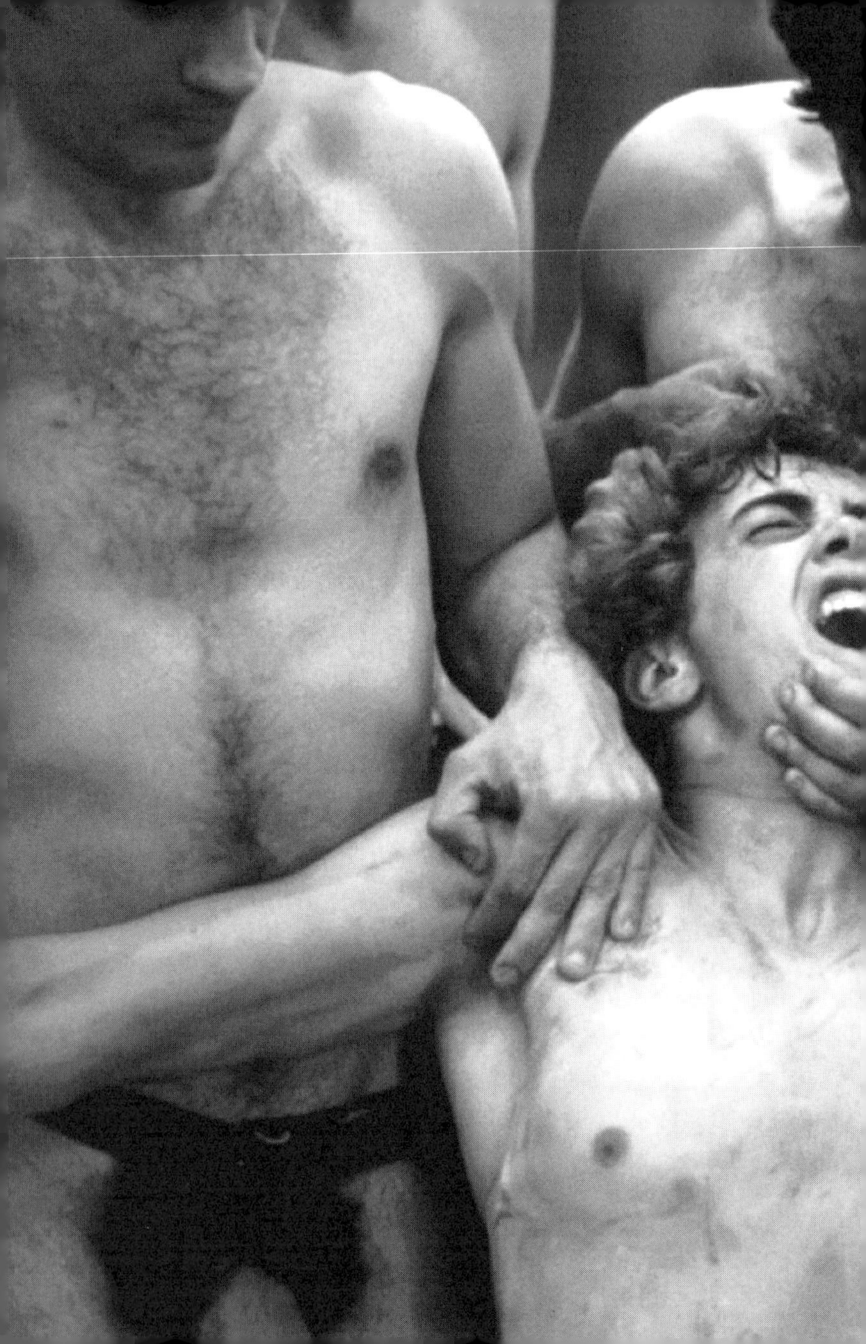

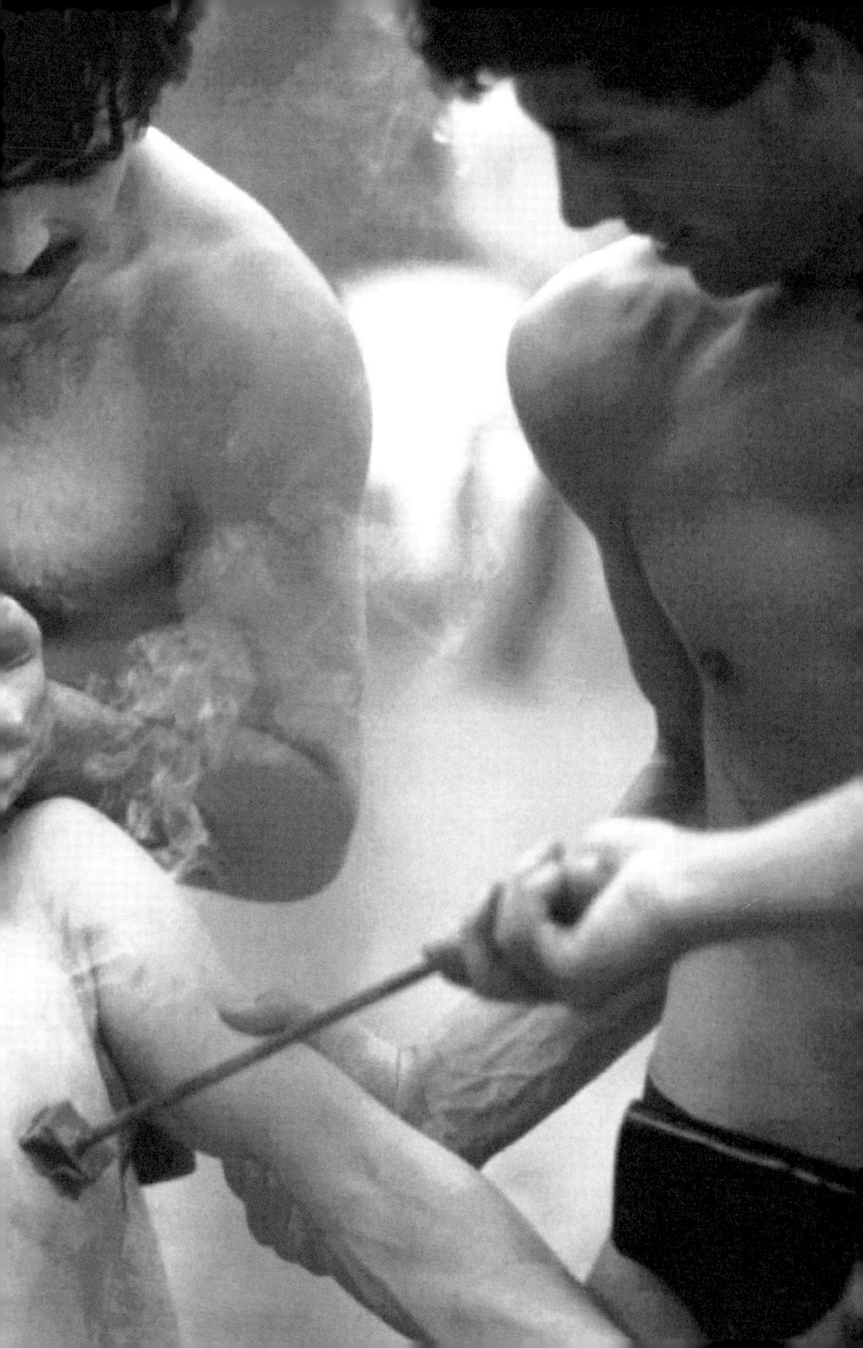

4.
Circle of Blood

Salò exerts a unique impact of violence and disruption on the viewer's eye, exploring a ground of extreme sensorial disruption more usually associated with non-narrative experimental cinema. The film adroitly manoeuvres the viewer's perspective between that of the victim and that of the torturer, finally situating the viewer firmly in the torture-seat. In *Salò*, the viewer is positioned firmly on the side of monstrosity, and then has a long way back to travel, corporeally and mentally, at the end of the film, if the decision is taken to repudiate that position.

In the final part of *120 Days of Sodom*, Sade's story-tellers range over a vast ground of dismemberment, disembowelment, torture and human eradication, while the libertines, incited by those narratives, perform concurrent acts of torture and killing. Sade's story-tellers recount an entire catalogue of bestiality, some instances of which appear to have been a source of prefiguring inspiration for the performance-acts of the Vienna Action Group: 'This libertine fucks a turkey whose head is gripped between the thighs of a nude, prostrate girl, so it appears he is buggering her. As he pumps away his valet sodomizes him without mercy, and at the moment he ejaculates, the girl slits the turkey's throat.'[6] Many of Sade's narrated acts form spectacular performances which evidently have their source in medieval strategies of torture and execution, but also work to compact rituals of killing with obsessional sodomy.

At the end of *120 Days of Sodom*, a careful accounting is made by Sade of the previous four months, detailing the eradication of the children and the numbers of story-tellers and 'cockmongers' who have survived the event. That final calculation is in contrast to the description of the children's intricate slaughter which, even in the fragmentary, unfinished state of Sade's manuscript, always contains minute, lavish detail: 'Next Giton is dragged forth; a burning bodkin is driven through the end of his cock, his remaining testicle is impaled with needles, and four of his teeth gouged out with chisels. Then comes Zelmire, whose death is not far off; a hot poker is run deep into her cunt, six gaping gashes are carved into her tits, and each master pummels her face twenty times with a gloved fist. They rip out four teeth and explode one eye with a skewer, whipping and buggering her for good measure.'[7] The viewer of *Salò,* positioned explicitly by Pasolini into the viewpoint of the binocular-wielding succession of libertines, experiences more fragmentary sequences; the killings of the boys and girls, in the courtyard of the villa, oscillate from close-ups to long-shots, in a volatile rhythm. The acts of slaughter are clearly drawn in large part from those which Pasolini himself had heard of or witnessed in the final stages of the Italian fascist forces' hold on power in 1944-45, and which were common punishments for civilians' acts of support for the partisans: eye-gougings, torture with fire, and anal-rapes followed by execution by hanging. Pasolini's last act in *Salò* is to cut from the slaughter to a tender encounter between two of the young fascists guarding the villa: the two male youths (one of whom is played by Claudio Tròccoli, Pasolini's final lover) dance obliviously, as music from the radio plays.

Pasolini's own violent last act took place seven months after he had filmed that final shot of *Salò*. Many of his friends rejected the official conclusion that he had been battered to death by a lone hustler, and believed instead that he was murdered, in the night of 1-2 November 1975, by agents of the corrupt Italian Christian Democratic Party government, in collusion with neofascist elements; at that time, very little investigation was conducted by the Italian police into Pasolini's killing, and much of the forensic evidence from the site of his death had soon mysteriously disappeared. Thirty years later, it was confirmed by the successors of that government that, from the end of the 1960s until the beginning of the 1980s, at a time of considerable social tension in Italy, it had been covertly organizing and inciting acts of terrorism and of murder, with the aim of terrifying and subjugating the Italian population into supporting that government's repressive, right-wing agenda, against which Pasolini had fiercely protested. As yet, however, no confirmation has ever been made that Pasolini's killing was executed or directly 'facilitated' by the Italian government or its neofascist associates.

Three weeks after Pasolini had completed the editing of *Salò*, and on the day after he had returned to Rome from Paris, where he had worked on the film's French-language version, he picked up a seventeen-year-old hustler, Giuseppe Pelosi, late on the evening of 1 November 1975, outside Rome's Stazione Termini central railway-station. On the afternoon of that same day, Pasolini had given his final interview, noting: 'In a certain sense, we are all weak because we are all victims. And are guilty because all are ready for the massacre game...'.[8] Pasolini offered Pelosi the modest sum of twenty thousand lire, and then drove him in his Alfa Romeo Giulia 2000 sports-car to isolated waste-ground near the sea at Ostia, to the west of Rome, where Pasolini sucked the boy's penis, with the two men still seated in the car. After Pasolini and Pelosi had exited the car to continue their sex act in the wasteland, Pasolini was abruptly attacked, and had his penis and testicles kicked with such violence that he suffered a severe internal haemorrhage; he then had his head clubbed so savagely with a wooden plank that his skull burst open, and brain-matter stuck to the plank. As he lay on the ground, he had his upper body driven-over by his own car, and died instantly from (as the autopsy stated) 'tearing-apart of the chest' (his heart literally burst under the pressure of the car's weight) and the crushing of his skull. The hustler Pelosi then drove off in the stolen car, stopped at a water-fountain in Ostia to wash Pasolini's blood from his clothes, and then sped off on the highway towards Rome in an exhilarated frenzy; he was almost immediately arrested and detained by the police for speeding, and confessed to the killing later that day. Pasolini had remained where he fell until he was discovered on the wasteland at dawn, on his front, one arm trapped under his body, his chest and skull almost flattened-down to the level of the ground, a foot-wide pool of congealed blood like a mythic halo around his head.

At Pelosi's trial, it was finally decided that he had acted alone. But the severity of the attack on Pasolini indicated the likelihood that Pelosi had been working in collaboration with four of his hustler-associates from the Stazione Termini, with whom he had talked briefly, at the railway-station's bar, before then leaving for the Ostia wasteland with Pasolini. The group of five hustlers may have attacked Pasolini simply in order to rob him, or the killing may have been a kind of initiation-ceremony for Pelosi (many of the Stazione Termini hustlers were murderous thugs, and carried greater prestige after having accomplished their first act of killing), in which Pasolini had the misfortune to be the 'old faggot' who was in the wrong place at the wrong time; in that scenario, the other four hustlers drove separately to Ostia, trailing the Alfa Romeo Giulia 2000 sports-car carrying Pasolini and Pelosi, and then all five hustlers attacked Pasolini together, holding him down to beat his head with the plank. Although Pasolini was over fifty, he remained tough and muscled from his regular football-games, so it was unlikely that one young hustler alone could have inflicted so much damage to his body. Pelosi served seven years of a nine-year prison-sentence for the murder; after his release in 1983, he undertook a career as a criminal, committing robberies and acts of violence, and gave magazine and television interviews about his role in Pasolini's killing; he never admitted the participation of other hustlers in the murder, and, in recent years, even denied his own involvement.

A final scenario, raised by Pasolini's more pessimistic friends at the time of his death, was the possibility of an intentional suicide, orchestrated by Pasolini himself, in his despair at the dissipation, by 1975, of the 1960s' riotous momentum towards revolutionary social change, and the onset of a terminally consumerist, media-dominated Italian society, which increasingly mocked and dismissed Pasolini's work.

Whether Pasolini was murdered by the Italian government's agents and neofascist associates, by one hustler alone, or by five hustlers together, or as a result of his own suicidal desire, the story of his killing, in the end, is reduced to the status of Sade's bare, notational narrative-fragments in Parts Two to Four of *120 Days of Sodom.* The account given of that killing by Pelosi's trial-judge (a lenient judge, like Sade himself), drawing from Pelosi's testimony, resonates with the relentless narrational momentum of Sade's story-tellers at the Castle of Silling: 'Pelosi added that Pasolini brought him to the playing field; that Pasolini took Pelosi's penis in his mouth for a moment but did not finish the blow-job; that he made Pelosi get out of the car and came up behind him, squeezing him from behind and trying to lower his trousers; that Pelosi told him to stop and instead Pasolini picked up a stake of the kind used for garden-fences and tried to put it up his behind, or at least he stuck it against his behind though without even lowering his trousers; that Pelosi turned around and told him he was crazy; that Pasolini by now was without his glasses, which he had left in the car, and on looking him in the face it seemed to Pelosi so much the face of a madman that he was frightened; that he tried to run but stumbled and fell; that he felt Pasolini on top of him, hitting him on the head with a stick; that he grabbed the stick and flung Pasolini away from him; that he again started running, and again was caught and struck on the temple and various parts of the body; that he noticed a plank on the ground, picked it up and broke it over Pasolini's head; that he also kicked him once or twice "in the balls"; that Pasolini seemed not even to feel those kicks; that then Pasolini grabbed him and struck him again on the nose; that Pelosi no longer saw what he was doing and repeatedly hit Pasolini with the plank until he heard him wheezing to the ground; that he ran in the direction of the car carrying the two broken pieces of plank and the stake, which he threw away near the car; that he got immediately into the car and fled in it; that he did not know whether or not in his escape he had run over Pasolini's body with the car... and that during these events, he and Pasolini had always been alone.'[9]

In his death, and in his final act as a film-maker with *Salò*, Pier Paulo Pasolini confirmed a definitive declaration he had made in an interview several years earlier: 'I love life fiercely, desperately. And I believe that this fierceness, this desperation will carry me to the end... How will it all end? I don't know.'[10]

Notes

1. Stack, Oswald, *Pasolini on Pasolini*, Thames and Hudson, (London), 1969, pp.55-56.

2. Siciliano, Enzo, *Pasolini*, Bloomsbury (London), 1987, p.386.

3. Marquis de Sade, *120 Days of Sodom*, Solar Books (Washington DC), 2008, p.21.

4. Pasolini, interview with Gideon Bachmann from April 1975, 'Pasolini on De Sade', *Film Quarterly* (Berkeley), issue of Winter 1975-76, p.41.

5. ibid, p.41.

6. *120 Days of Sodom*, p.248.

7. ibid, p.284.

8. Pasolini, interview with Furio Colombo, from the afternoon of 1 November 1975, for the newspaper arts supplement 'Tutto libro' (Turin), quoted in Schwartz, Barth David, *Pasolini Requiem*, Pantheon, New York, 1992, p.649.

9. *Pasolin*i, pp.8-9.

10. ibid (interview with the French magazine *Lui*, April 1970), p.359.

IV
JOE D'AMATO AND SADE: THE ART OF LOVE

Introduction

Alongside the infamous Jesus Franco, Italian exploitation director Joe D'Amato (real name Aristide Massaccesi) can also rightly claim the label of being a 'sadean' filmmaker. This definition is applicable not merely because much of D'Amato's output circulated within the domain of the 'pornographic'. Rather, it is the fact that his narratives were marked by a type of cross-generic overload, which combined outrageous doses of sex and horror in an appeal to different 'grindhouse' audiences. The extreme nature of many of D'Amato's crossover productions can be inferred by a brief consideration of some of his most notorious titles. These centred on macabre depictions of sex which saw zombies attacking Westerners with monstrous phalluses (*Porno Holocaust*, 1979), as well as voodoo priestesses castrating their lovers at the point of orgasm (*Erotic Nights Of The Living Dead*, 1980). Other outrageous scenes of sexual trauma that D'Amato constructed included those featuring repressed taxidermists seducing young women in the same bed as their dead brides (*Beyond The Darkness*) as well as sexually charged couples who copulate before images of filmed female mutilation (*Emanuelle In America*, 1976), as well as the juxtaposition of sex and bloody cannibalism in *Emanuelle And The Last Cannibals* (1977) or *Papaya: Love Goddess Of The Cannibals* (1978).

What united all of these productions was D'Amato's unflinching fusion of sex and gore. This clearly drew on Sade's favoured combination of eroticism and violence, to the extent that the boundaries of sexual desire and displeasure were dissolved. For instance, writing in his recent book *Sade: The Libertine Novels*, John Phillips has defined works such as *120 Days Of Sodom* as dominated by "a criminal orgy of sexual deviance protracted well beyond the normal limits of human endurance."[1]

At the level of film form, D'Amato's fusion of disparate generic elements also affected the logical structure of his works. These were marked by a repetitious, meandering and often illogical structure that frequently outraged many of the director's detractors. However, these strategies also recall the contradictory nature of narrative excess and deviation found in Sade's work. As Maurice Charney has noted, "Sade's gargantuan sexual imagination is not intended to provoke or inflame desire; rather the vast repetition has a numbing effect."[2] It is precisely such a numbing effect, which accompanied the erotic and macabre crossover imagery in Joe D'Amato's work.

While the sadean influences are clear in both the form and content of Joe D'Amato's delirious 1970s productions, little comment has been made on the 35mm hardcore films with which he became involved be from 1994 until his death in 1999. For many, these glossy, 'feel good' porn productions, (whose titles included *X-Hamlet* [1994], *Barone Von Masoch* [1994] and *Tarzan-X Shame Of Jane* [1994]), seem to share little connection with the director's earlier, controversial output.

However, by considering two porn titles from D'Amato's late career: *120 Days Of The Anal* (1995) and *The Marquis De Sade* (1995), I wish show an essential 'Sadean continuity' between these texts and the director's infamous earlier output. It is not merely the fact that these two films take the figure of Sade and his philosophy as their focus, rather they retain the director's interest in emphasising the horrific nature of sexuality, while also presenting these images in a convoluted and repetitive narrative form. In order to identify these features, I want to firstly offer a case study drawn from D'Amato's seventies output before considering its links to his later hardcore productions.

Sadean Sex In The Seventies

Several of the sadean thematic and stylistic structures with which Joe D'Amato first gained international exposure (and notoriety) are evident in his 1976 film *Emanuelle And Francoise.* This production (literally) recounts the fatal coupling between a manipulative womaniser named Carlo (played by D'Amato's scriptwriter George Eastman), and two sisters: Francoise and Emanuelle. The narrative is organised around a disorientating number of flashbacks that detail the catalogue of sexual humiliations forced upon the virginal Francoise by Carlo, resulting in her eventual suicide. These fatal actions are later revealed to the more sexually liberated Emanuelle, in the form of a suicide note penned by Francoise before she jumped to her death under a speeding train. The document, which reveals that Carlo forced his lover to appear in pornographic movies against her will (as well as coercing her into sexual encounters with a number of his business associates) becomes the trigger upon which Emanuelle plots a violent revenge against the male protagonist.

After orchestrating a meeting with Carlo, the heroine manipulates his sexual interest in her, inviting the character to her home with the promises of seduction. Emanuelle then drugs Carlo and when the protagonist awakes, he finds that he has been imprisoned behind a two-way mirror. From this position of incarceration, Carlo is forced to watch Emanuelle engage in a number of sexual liaisons with male and female partners (including his current girlfriend, Mira).

Via the heroine's revenge plot, *Emanuelle and Francoise* renders the thrill of sexual excess and display as a source of humiliation and trauma. Not only does Emanuelle proceed to starve, torture, threaten to kill and castrate her captive, but she also uses drugs to further disorientate and traumatise him. For instance, one hallucinogenic scene features Carlo imagining that he is witnessing a refined dinner party that ends in a bizarre cannibalistic orgy.

In its theme and arrangement, *Emanuelle And Francoise* embodies many of the traits of Sadean fiction as described by critics such as Maurice Charney. For instance, its separation of female protagonists into virginal and sexual types clearly recalls Sade's classic division of virtue and vice in the duel female figures of Justine and Juliette, with the distinction between regimes of sexual power (and powerlessness) that this implies. For instance, Carlo's exploitation of the emotionally laden and vulnerable Francoise is juxtaposed and contrasted to his exploitation *by* the erotically charged Emanuelle. This division between virgin and vamp draws parity with the distinction that Charney makes between "Justine's virginal passivity and Juliette's sexual terror."

D'Amato even manipulates the film's convoluted narrative structure as a way of drawing distinctions between his two heroines. For instance, the opening credit scene of the film reveals Francoise stripping confidently before a cameraman in what appears to be a consensual 'glamour' photography shoot. It is only the later discovery of the heroine's suicide note that reveals Carlo's coercion of the protagonist into these pornographic scenarios against her will. Carlo's treatment of Francoise indicates in the words of Leo Charney that "all sex in Sade is a form of tyranny, by which the dominant partner imposes his will on the subservient sex object."[3] This serves to distinguish the fate of the heroine from the subsequent actions of Emanuelle, who by subverting Carlo's control over the sexual scenario places him in the very masochistic position previously enforced on her sister. Within the realm of Sadean aesthetics, the film's constantly changing set of power dynamics indicates that all sexual relations "are sadomasochistic ones, with the possibility that roles can be temporarily changed for the purposes of experimentation."[4]

However, is not merely the oscillation between states of power and oppression that underlie the Sadean impetus in *Emanuelle And Francoise*. Rather, it is the film's very obsession with *seeing* its protagonists *perform* the sexual act that translates its erotic acts into scenarios of theatrical display. Here, sex is relocated from a private into a public act, echoing what John Phillips has termed as the essentially "public and theatrical" nature of Sade's writing.[5] As with novels like *The 120 Days Of Sodom*, D'Amato's film produces sexual activity staged before an audience, whose outcomes liable to evoke a number of contradictory and uncomfortable emotions.

This capacity for erotic satisfaction to be transmuted into a scenario of suffering is indicated in the film's opening segment. Here, a montage sequence offers the illusion of a content Francoise shopping for a variety of gifts for Carlo on her way home from the glamour photography shoot. Although these scenes establish an up-beat theme to the proceedings, they are suddenly disrupted when she arrives home to discover Carlo making love to another woman. Watching the erotic encounter through a door opening, Francoise adopts the position of the classic D'Amato voyeur: that is a protagonist whose obsession with looking overrides the traumatic potential for what is actually viewed.[6] (If it is the case that D'Amato's 'lookers' assume a fatalistic and masochistic position, then this structure finds its logical conclusion in Carlo's positioning as the bound/tortured voyeur in the final stages of the film).

While this rendering of sexual activity as a site of public spectacle provides a motivating principle for *Emanuelle And Francoise,* it also constructs of point of traumatic repetition around which the narrative revolves. Although the heroine dies within the first five minutes of the film, her suicide note effectively keeps her alive, as well as prolonging her past tense suffering via a series of extended flashbacks. These shifts in filmic tense added to the narrative's already convoluted structure, much to the confusion of many contemporary reviewers. For instance, David Badder derided the structure of the narrative as "deadly dull"; concluding that it was guaranteed to send the bulk of its "frustrated audience into a deep sleep long before its predictable denouement."[7]

It is precisely because of these criticisms, that the structure of D'Amato's film can be viewed within the sadean tradition. Here, narrative structure is used as a form of experimentation, duplication and deviation that frequently works at odds with the erotic impact that the content attempts to create. Writing in *Sade: The Libertine Novels*, John Phillips has noted that the repetitive and self-referential comments about *how* the libertine orgies of *One Hundred and Twenty Days of Sodom* are being staged and executed produces a diminishing of "erotic impact on the reader."[8] As Phillips comments:

"Overall... *Les 120 Journées* functions inefficiently as a work of pornography, since as we have seen, the reader's interest is constantly displaced from any erotic effect to the ways in which sexuality is represented through linguistic, arithmetical and other formal structures."[9]

While the unsettling combination of titillation and trauma packaged in a monotonous, alienating form link D'Amato's seventies work to the effect that Phillips describes, these features are also present in the director's later hardcore productions which deal explicitly with the figure of Sade and his ideas.

Lust In A Loop: The Role Of Repetition In "120 Days Of The Anal"

Produced as an Italian/American co-production, *120 Days Of The Anal* (aka *Anal Palace*) appears as the more 'restrained' of the 'Sadean' films that films that Joe D'Amato completed in 1995. The film translates Sade's victimised heroine Justine in to the figure of Martine, who is imprisoned and molested by a group of lusty servants in the film's opening. Her fate is secured by the sudden intervention of an unnamed libertine (played by porn icon Marc Davis). The hero persuades the assembled males that their erotic satisfaction will be heightened through their victim's compliance, arguing that he will be able to 'seduce' her into submission with tales of the libertine orgies he has organised. At first, Davis' plan is greeted with derision, with one of the assembled males sneering that one "cannot fuck with your eyes", after being asked to assume the position of voyeur.

While Martine's gradual and increasingly sexualised writhing convinces the crowd of the libertine's scheme, it also underscores the fact that any subsequent erotic 'adventures' will be premised upon the unpalatable outcome of Martine's impending abuse. While the more disturbing aspects of the libertine's plan are softened by the 'consensual' nature of the film's pornographic motifs, it also functions as a basis of sexual trauma upon which the narrative continually returns. Equally, in Davis' re-organisation of the male crowd into a gathering of sexual gazers, the film demonstrates the centrality of voyeurism and exhibitionistic display within the Sadean setting. For Maurice Charney, in these scenarios, "Sex is theatricalised in Sade, and the orgy is his most natural form of sexual experience."[10] This point is demonstrated through the several flashback scenes through which Davis recounts his debauched past.

Here, at least two of the four extended sex scenes play upon vision (and indeed a lack of sight) as being a precursor to erotic excitement. For instance, the second flashback scene features a group of masked men who have to guess the identity of their female sexual partners by the smell of their body fluids, before an orgy ensues. Equally, the third flashback sequence features a hooded female who is at first offered to the assembled male libertines before being ravished by the group's well-endowed black servant. During the sequence, D'Amato's camera appears as if concealed behind plants and bushes, (before focusing more fully on the sexual acts depicted), a strategy that once again underscores the voyeuristic potential inherent in the libertine regime.

Even when the film is not shifting its male and female protagonists through regimes of voyeurism/concealed sight, the impetus to *look* is central to the staging of the sex scenes as a sight of public spectacle. For instance, one of the final flashbacks from *120 Days Of The Anal* features a female engaged in an act of masturbation before the libertine crowd organised in a circular pattern around her. As the scene unfolds, Davis and his black servant join her in an act of vaginal and anal intercourse. Rather

than enter the coupling, the rest of the assembled group find gratification in their roles as voyeurs, leading to several shots of male and female self-pleasuring. Through these scenes, *120 Days Of The Anal* confirms Sade's view of the erotic act as a communal affair. As John Phillips has noted, for Sade sex is "both public and theatrical... debauchery here is above all a shared activity in which to be seen is as important as to see."[11]

In its use of features such as the traumatic basis to sexual activity, as well as a voyeuristic obsession with erotic events, *120 Days Of The Anal* draws clear connections with not only the philosophy of Sade, but also the earlier output of Joe D'Amato. The film's connection with both of these sources is also confirmed through the repetitive shifting between the flashback and present tense scenes that make up the structure of the film. *120 Days Of The Anal* is constructed around four key flashback scenes, which are alternated with shots of Martine's increasing sexual frenzy as Davis recounts the tales. What is noticeable about this structuring process is the way in which duration alters to mirror the heroine's increasing sexual excitement. While the first two flashbacks are of similar length, the final ones occupy a much shorter time-span, being fragmented by D'Amato's brief return to Martine's approaching sexual climax.

However, if the structure of the film is constructed around the frenzied drive towards orgasm, this does not necessarily guarantee the sexual release and satisfaction that the term may imply. Rather, it condemns the viewer to type of formal alienation, similar to the effect that John Phillips has identified in Sade's writings. Here, the constant alternation between differing cinematic tenses robs the spectator of the necessary temporal (and frequently visual) anchors from which to secure a position of gratification. If this is a result of the repetitive and convoluted form in which sexual activity takes place, then its disengaging effect is heightened by the way in which D'Amato frames the sexual activity of the libertine's recollections. Whereas Martine's sexual excitement is shot from an overhead position (allowing the viewer access to the whole of her body), the libertine encounters are framed in such extreme close-up that a 'genital vignette' replaces total, human interaction.

Via this method, the camera gazes in extreme proximity on a succession of penis, vagina and anus shots, which prove more alienating that arousing to the viewer. This is particularly marked in the 'group' encounters that dominate the first two flashbacks. Here, the camera frequently switches between differing sets of sex organs without identifying their respective owners. In so doing, D'Amato's film provokes a curious barrier between the audience and the sexual excesses it depicts. This provides a visual equivalent of the "derealising" effect that John Phillips has identified in Sade's literary works. Here, textual complexity and ambiguity "focuses attention on process rather than erotic content."[12]

Titillation And Torture: Rocco And His Brother

With *120 Days Of The Anal*, D'Amato gestures towards the repetition of traumatic/sexual encounters that were evident in his seventies productions. His 1995 companion piece *The Marquis De Sade* makes these links even more explicit, by taking Sade's own incarceration as its central subject matter. In many respects, the film shares the complicated formal structure of earlier D'Amato works such as *Emanuelle And Francoise*. Here, Donatien's fall from grace is depicted within a series of extended flashbacks that are fragmented by sudden (and often unmotivated) shifts in filmic tense.

From the outset, D'Amato makes good use of a doubling motif to initiate the flashback sequences. Here, the imprisoned Marquis finds his past actions challenged by an imaginary incarnation of himself. Both Sade and his chastising double are played by the famed Italian porn stud (and D'Amato regular) Rocco Siffredi. This iconic male performer gained expose on the adult circuit for not only the excessive size of his penis (as well as its ejaculating capacities), but also his well toned, body-building physique. However, in contrast to his usually fine-tuned appearance, D'Amato casts him here as a gaunt figure who is wracked by the demons of his past.

As with D'Amato's earlier incarnation of Carlo the voyeur, this is a figure whose reflections and sexual obsessions are a source of displeasure rather than guaranteeing sexual satisfaction. The traumatic basis to the protagonist's malaise is indicated in the film's first flashback, when the Marquis' double asks him to recollect "his first discovery of the female sex." The flashback that follows, features the camera adopting a point of view style, whilst concealed within a closet. From this position, a subjective perspective is given watching a young maid disrobe. When the illicit gazer (revealed as a childhood Sade) is discovered, it is interesting to that it is the camera lens itself that is directly reprimanded, being beaten and shaken by the semi-naked women. Thus it can be argued that it is not only the protagonist, but also the viewer (beyond the limits of the film frame), who come to share Sade's humiliation. Such images confirm that in the Sadean universe, sexuality is linked to despair and mistreatment rather than physical liberation. In the words of Maurice Charney:

"Sade is a spokesman for hard and difficult sex, violent, cruel and energetic. Orgasm unites man with the animal creation and is a kind of epileptic fit or temporary seizure by which we abandon all pretensions to reason and false enlightenment. Against a benevolent and optimistic romanticism, Sade opposes a negative, primitive, chaotic and destructive view of the sexual relationship."[13]

Although the latter flashback scenes recounting the activities of the adult Sade show him in a dominating position over his varied female partners, they must be premised upon the initial scene of violence and humiliation enacted against the protagonist. (As well as the character's torment from his imaginary divided self in the present tense scenes punctuating these sexual encounters).[14] Equally, even those scenes which feature Sade orchestrating the sexual humiliation of others feature an act of voyeurism on the part of an aroused on-looker, thereby connecting them with the perils of voyeurism identified in D'Amato's earlier work.

An example of such a scenario can be found in the second flashback scene featuring the adult Sade. Here, Renée, (the Marquis' future bride) conceals herself and watches with a mixture of passion and disgust as the libertine coerces a prostitute into a series of couplings that are intended to degrade. Firstly, Sade attempts to placate his new partner with promises of gold coins, before making her crouch down and urinate over the reward on offer. When her bladder skills are revealed as too inadequate to arouse the libertine, he gestures the prostitute towards an act of oral sex before urinating over her face and hair.

The anal sex scene between the pair that follows retains these overtones of violence and sexual oppression. Firstly, Sade enters his partner roughly from behind before threatening to "rip your guts out". The extended scenes of anality that follow are similarly coded within a vocabulary of disgust. Here, the libertine

claims that he will slice his partner's "ass open" as well as "pull the shit out of her".[15] The sex scene ends when Sade reaches a sexual climax while attempting to use his penis to choke his conquest at the point of orgasm. In many respects, this body fluid-dominated sex scene draws comparison with some of the more extreme orgies enacted in *120 Days of Sodom*. These featured:

> "...other transgressive acts... promptly enacted by the libertines include urine-drinking, armpit smelling, saliva swallowing, fart swallowing, nostril licking, the drinking of menstrual blood, and of course, fucking."[16]

Arguably, the power behind these otherwise offensive scenarios lies in the ability to use the body (and its waste products) as a way of introducing an element of displeasure into an otherwise titillating scenario.[17] As has already been established, this feature is a long established trait in D'Amato's films. In *The Marquis De Sade*, the strategy of rendering pornographic 'thrills' distasteful is most marked in the sequence where two women are blindfolded before being required to arouse an unidentified suitor. Although Sade informs his sightless assistants that they are "licking the body of a young athlete from head to foot", when their vision is restored they are as disgusted to find that they have been cavorting with an overweight, deformed, middle-aged servant. Although the women verbalise their displeasure upon this discovery, and even struggle against nausea at the sight of the servant's dwarfish genitals, Sade coerces them to a climax with this unlikely partner. Here, the pleasure of sexual release is overburdened by a sense of decay and disgust. This once again mirrors the literary source material upon which D'Amato draws. As John Phillips has noted, rather than just offend the senses, Sade uses such repulsive imagery to invert "aesthetic norms, replacing the sweet fragrances of youth and beauty with the foul smelling and ugly as a basis of sexual attraction".[18]

Titillation And Trauma: Rocco And His Body

Through their traumatic rendering of sex with violence, degradation or implied threat, the later films of Joe D'Amato can be aligned with the Sadean impetus that defined his most infamous output of the seventies. These texts also display the Sadean obsessions with voyeurism and erotic exhibitionism that defined works such as *120 Days of Sodom.* Equally, the formal structure of D'Amato's works, with their emphasis on repetition and deviation can be seen as similar to the narrative experiments that critics such as Phillips and Charney have identified in Sade's fiction.

In conclusion, it is also worth considering the extent to which this overlap between titillation and trauma might affect depictions of masculinity within a format that has traditionally been seen as gratifying male desires. As Peter Lehman has noted, through its conventions, motifs and modes of depiction, mainstream heterosexual pornography seeks to provoke a distinct split between the genders, while attributing erotic power to the male. This is seen in frequency with which male characters function as unchecked voyeurs: i.e. they have visual access to the naked female body by watching from a secret location. Equally, as Lehman notes, by focusing on the male orgasm (or 'money shot') as a guarantor of sexual satisfaction, such genre conventions confirm that:

"Male sexuality lies at the centre of the porn genre. Everything turns on affirming and satisfying male desires and the hard-core scene typically ends immediately after the visual proof that this has occurred. Women's pleasure becomes merely a sign of their dependence on the phallus."[19]

By fusing sex with violence, threat and disgust, both Sade and D'Amato's work can be seen as reversing many of the male-centred conventions of pornography. From Carlo's status as impotent, imprisoned gazer in *Emanuelle And Francoise*, to the beating attributed to the visually curious youngster (and viewer) in the opening of *The Marquis De Sade*, these works introduce a generically uncharacteristic degree of punishment associated with male voyeurism. Alongside this denigration of gendered looking, D'Amato reverses the 'invisibility' often associated with modes of male display in such formats.

While it is true that women still occupy a position of visual spectacle in both his early and later erotic dramas, it is noticeable that their exhibitionistic role is in fact superseded by an obsessive focus on the male body. An example of this strategy can be seen in the first flashback featuring Rocco Siffredi as the adult Sade. Here, the protagonist is depicted as bathing while being secretly watched by two giggling chambermaids. When the females are discovered, they are invited to join the bather and an orgy ensues. What is interesting about the sexual acts that unfold here is the way in which the camera glides over the images of the females undressing (traditionally the focus of such porno explorations), coming to rest instead on shots of Sade's penis and buttocks.[20]

Rather than representing an isolated example, it can be argued that a visual obsession with Rocco Siffredi's body dominates both this sex scene as well as the other erotic encounters in *The Marquis De Sade*. While it is not uncommon for such iconic (and well-endowed) male porn performers to attract a high degree of visual interest, these strategies of display work in opposition to the normal conventions of masculine display within pornography. As Peter Lehman has noted in the book *Running Scared: Masculinity and Representations of the Male Body*, when reduced to a site of naked spectacle, images of masculinity evoke a number of contradictory (and potentially threatening) emotions in the heterosexual man. As a result, these have to be minimised by anchoring such scenes of exhibitionism to the primary goal of servicing the depicted women. Here, as "women desire the visibility of male ejaculation, they frequently express their desire for large penises."[21]

In contrast to these 'traditional' uses of the male body in porn, D'Amato's depiction of Siffredi connotes a high degree of sexual ambiguity that denies the male viewer a stable point of masculine identification. These sexual tensions are evidenced in the scene where an experienced lesbian inducts a younger woman into the pleasures of same sex copulation, which she claims requires a rejection of "the strong, muscular arms of a male." After informing the sexual novice that De Sade's new maid will be joining them, an unidentified 'woman' appears and is initiated into the coupling. However, as the pair begins to disrobe the dress of their new partner, they are surprised to find that is in fact Sade, who has disguised himself as a woman in order to join in the encounter. He then proceeds to initiate intercourse while still wearing his 'female' wig, earrings, corset and heavily rouged face.[22]

While this degree of feminising the male 'erotic icon' is uncommon within the boundaries heterosexual pornography, it is characteristic of Sadean sexual ambiguity from which D'Amato draws his source material.[23] As John Phllips has noted, although novels like *120 Days of the Sodom* abound with phallic imagery, these depictions of masculinity are frequently accompanied by a degree of sexual fluidity. For instance, Phillips discusses the figure of the financier Durcet whom Sade has depicted as possessing "an incredibly small penis and the breasts and buttocks of a woman."[24]

The degree of sexual ambiguity found in Sade and D'Amato's work functions at the level of the iconic, whilst also affecting the way in which soundtrack connotes sexual pleasure. For critics like Peter Lehman, although the soundtracks in porn productions are geared towards the vocalisation of female pleasure, they function merely as a response to the genre's focus on dominant male desires. Here, "soundtrack editing further structures these moans to build with these visuals in a pattern geared to male sexual climax".[25] In contrast to these unambiguous anchors of male heterosexual activity, the soundtrack to works such as *The Marquis De Sade* is dominated by a type of male aural exhibitionism. This is exemplified by the high pitched screeching of Siffredi at the point of orgasm, or the effeminate squealing of his overweight, middle-aged assistant as he nears a sexual climax. These vocal gestures find parity with the construction of the Sadean heroes that John Phillips has studied. As evidenced in novels such as *120 Days of Sodom,* these are libertines, who while gendered male, are seen to "shriek like banshees when reaching orgasm."[26] The evidence of these codes in the later films of Joe D'Amato, once again point to the way in which the filmmaker utilised the ideas and imagery of the Marquis de Sade to upset the patterns and presumptions within the pornographic text.

Notes

1. John Phillips, Sade: *The Libertine Novels*. (London: Pluto Press, 2001), p.32.

2. Maurice Charney, *Sexual Fiction* (London: Methuen & Co, 1981), p.35.

3. Ibid., p.34.

4. Ibid., p.34.

5. John Phillips, p.43.

6. During the scene, the camera pans between Francoise's horrified gaze, Carlos's erotic coupling and a small statue that adorns a bedside cabinet. The figure, with distorted features and oversized, leering eyes in many respects echoes the near-monstrous status that D'Amato gives his voyeurs in the film.

7. David Badder, *Emanuelle And Francoise* (review), *Monthly Film Bulletin*. V44. n526. November 1977 p.232.

8. Phillips, p.54.

9. Ibid., p.56.

10. Maurice Charney, p.33.

11.John Phillips, p.43.

12. Ibid., p.55.

13. Maurice Charney, p.38.

14. The lyrics of the film's theme tune 'Love and Pain' that accompany each of Sade's adult sexual encounters reiterates the connection between eroticism and displeasure that the film is trying to create.

15. The violence language of eroticism demonstrated in this scene is evident in an earlier coupling between Sade and two women, where the protagonist derides his partners with terms such as "bitch", "whore" and "pig".

16. John Phillips, p.51.

17. Another example conflating these contradictory emotions around the sex act occurs later in the film. Here, De Sade and his servant copulate in the same room as the female victims of the libertine's erotic experiments. The scene begins with Sade's assistant informing his master that he has prepared a dish of "girls well beaten" for dinner. The camera then pulls back to reveal two females who are bound to torture instruments as well as having been lacerated and bloodied in the course of their suffering. Sade then introduces two society women into the scene, and forces his sexual victims to watch this consensual coupling. The camera creates an uncomfortable effect by cutting from Siffredi's sexual actions to shots of the bound women who become increasingly aroused by their visual access to the proceedings. D'Amato's camera also concentrates on the blood dripping around the genital area of one victim, thus evoking the socially taboo imagery of menstrual blood that Phillips has identified in Sade's fiction.

18. Philllips, p.51-52.

19. Peter Lehman, *Running Scared: Masculinity and Representations of the Male Body* (Philadelphia: Temple University Press, 1993), 173.

20. A similar focus on male exhibitionism is also present in *120 Days Of The Anal.* For instance, during the libertine's first flashback recollection, the camera retards its focus on disrobing females in favour of extended shots of the muscular body of the black servant who comes to visually dominate the scene.

21. Lehman., p.174.

22. This scene indicates just one way in which D'Amato parodies the machismo associated with male porn stars. Another scene features a cameo by famed porn regular Christopher Clark, who is here cast as Sade's camp cousin who leaves one of his host's orgies after complaining that he can never get "himself any cock."

23. A similar degree of feminisation occurs to Marc Davis in the second flashback scene of *120 Days Of The Anal.* Here, D'Amato arranges the libertine in front of his (semi-naked) black servant during an encounter with an unidentified female. This close proximity between the two men gives the

appearance of a scene of homoerotic sex, normally shunned by mainstream heterosexual porn.

24. Phillips, p.37.

25. Lehman., p.178-179.

26. Phillips, p.37.

LIST OF ILLUSTRATIONS BY PAGE NUMBER:

COLOUR SECTION: